The 16 Career Clusters:
A Project-Based Orientation

SOUTH-WESTERN
CENGAGE Learning

Australia • Brazil • Japan • Korea • Mexico • Singapore • Spain • United Kingdom • United States

SOUTH-WESTERN
CENGAGE Learning

The 16 Career Clusters: A Project-Based Orientation

VP/Editorial Director: Jack W. Calhoun

VP/Editor-in-Chief: Karen Schmohe

Acquisitions Editor: Jane Congdon

VP/Marketing: Bill Hendee

Marketing Specialist: Linda Kuper

Production Manager: Patricia Matthews Boies

Content Project Manager: Corey Geissler

Manufacturing Coordinator: Kevin Kluck

Senior Art Director: Tippy McIntosh

Cover Designer: Craig Ramsdell

Fee Writers: Thomas N. Lewis, Cinci Stowell

For product information and technology assistance, contact us at **Cengage Learning Academic Resource Center, 1-800-423-0563**

For permission to use material from this text or product, submit all requests online at **www.cengage.com/permissions** Further permissions questions can be emailed to **permissionrequest@cengage.com**

Student Edition
ISBN-13: 978-0-538-44972-4
ISBN-10: 0-538-44972-1

Package with IMPACT CD-ROM
ISBN-13: 978-0-538-44971-7
ISBN-10: 0-538-44971-3

South-Western Cengage Learning
5191 Natorp Boulevard
Mason, OH 45040
USA

Cengage Learning products are represented in Canada by Nelson Education, Ltd.

For your course and learning solutions, visit **school.cengage.com**

The Career Clusters icons are being used with permission of the: States' Career Clusters Initiative, 2007, www.careerclusters.org

Printed in the United States of America
1 2 3 4 5 6 7 11 10 09 08

TABLE OF CONTENTS

TO THE STUDENT

Welcome to the world of job and career exploration! In this book you will learn about job and career possibilities by completing activities based on 16 Career Clusters.

The U.S. Office of Education has grouped careers into 16 different "Clusters" based on similar job characteristics. For example, the Law, Public Safety, Corrections & Security Cluster includes corrections officers, attorneys, park rangers, fire fighters, forensic specialists, and court reporters. These occupations may seem quite different, but many of the people who work at them have similar interests, skills, and personalities. Of course, occupations within a Cluster will vary depending on factors such as education, training, and work setting.

Career Clusters can help you connect what you learn in school—and what you already know--with the knowledge and skills you will need to succeed in a job. The Career Cluster approach allows you to explore a wide range of career opportunities from entry level through management and professional levels. In the process of completing this book, you will also learn more about your own talents and interests.

As you compete the 16 chapters in this book you will do research, use critical thinking and problem-solving skills, make ethical decisions, work with others, and practice skills you have learned in your math, science, social studies, and language arts courses.

Whether you know "what you want to be when you grow up" or haven't given careers a lot of thought yet, *The 16 Career Clusters: A Project-Based Orientation* will help you begin to identify occupations that interest you. You will not only learn *about* the jobs—in many activities, you will *try out* the job, performing the same kinds of tasks you would be assigned in the workplace.

In this book you will be invited to compare occupations in different Clusters. You will complete some activities by working with a partner or group. You will learn about—and make decisions about—hiring practices, business ethics, emerging technologies, finances, and globalization. Take your time completing the activities. Think about each job or career as it relates to you, your plans, and your dreams for the future.

Marketing, Sales & Service

Passions
- ☐ Organizing products
- ☐ Seeing the big picture
- ☐ Working with details

Attitude
- ☐ Outgoing
- ☐ Organized

Talents
- ☐ Communication skills
- ☐ Sociable
- ☐ Leadership abilities

Heart
- ☐ Likes to interact with people
- ☐ Likes to study people and trends

Some Career Areas to Consider
- ☐ Retail associate
- ☐ Buyer
- ☐ Warehouse manager
- ☐ E-commerce director
- ☐ Advertising manager

Employment Outlook
- ☐ Advertising, marketing, promotions, public relations and sales managers hold more than 700,000 jobs. Over 300,000 additional high-paying management positions are likely to be available over the next decade.
- ☐ Employment opportunities for retail salespeople are expected to be good.
- ☐ Individuals with a college degree or computer skills will be sought for managerial positions in sales, logistics, management information systems, marketing, and e-marketing.

ACTIVITY—PROFESSIONAL SALES AND MARKETING

The **close** is the step in a sale when the customer decides to buy a product or service. For many salespeople, this can be the hardest part of the sales process. Inexperienced salespeople are sometimes afraid to ask a customer to actually make a purchase! They are unsure of what to do if the customer says "No."

Effective salespeople understand that making a purchase—especially for an expensive item—can be difficult for a customer. Top salespeople also want to help their customers find the product or service that best meets their needs. Customers who feel they are being pressured into buying something will walk away. But if a salesperson can help the customer understand that the product or service meets an important need and offers a good value, then it is time to close the sale.

A salesperson can use many different techniques for closing a sale. The decision to buy should be made as easy as possible for the customer. The following are just a few examples of closing techniques:

☐ *Point out a benefit the customer values.* "This model is the most energy-efficient furnace on the market. Studies have shown that it can reduce your heating bill by 7 percent each month."

☐ *Offer a guarantee or extended trial.* "Why don't you buy these speakers and take them home for a couple of days. If you decide they don't sound right, just bring them back for a full refund."

☐ *Provide an "extra."* "If you purchase this suit, I'll throw in a tie at no extra charge."

☐ *Make payment convenient.* "We'd be happy to take your check, or we could go with that 12-month financing plan we talked about earlier."

☐ *Offer a choice.* "The white and grey are both in stock. Which would you like?"

☐ *Stress availability.* "If you order today, I'll have someone in your home for installation tomorrow afternoon."

Closing techniques are not tricks used by scheming salespeople to manipulate customers into buying something they don't really want or need. Closing is a skill that salespeople use to lead people to make decisions that are right for them. When customers make a purchase, they want to feel they have acted wisely; but sometimes customers are unsure about their decision. Good closing techniques can move customers past their doubts.

Directions: Use the information from the article and your own experiences to answer the following questions.

1. **Identifying** What is a *close* and when is it used in a sales presentation?

_____

_____

_____

_____

2. **Describing** How do effective salespeople treat their customers?

_____

_____

_____

_____

_____

3. **Evaluating** Which of the closing techniques in the article would be effective with a customer who is unsure if she can afford an item?

_____

_____

_____

_____

4. **Thinking Critically** Suppose you sell home theater systems. A customer is interested in a particular system, but tells you that he doesn't think he knows how to install it. Develop a closing technique to use with this customer.

_____

_____

_____

_____

5. **Analyzing** The best salespeople do not use closing techniques to manipulate customers into buying. But some do. Have you ever dealt with a salesperson using "hard sell" tactics? How did this make you feel? Did you buy the item?

_____

_____

_____

_____

6. **Assessing** Based on the article, what kinds of personal characteristics does a good salesperson need? How many of these characteristics do _you_ have?

_____

_____

_____

_____

ORGANIZING CAREER CHOICES

Directions: Choose one of the following occupations from the Marketing, Sales & Service Cluster: telemarketer, merchandise buyer, trade show manager, distribution coordinator, webmaster, or brand manager. Then use the following table to compare and contrast it with an occupation from another Career Cluster of your choice. Finally, tell which job would suit you best. Conduct library/Internet research to locate the necessary information.

Hint: The *Occupational Outlook Handbook* (OOH) is available in most public libraries and is a good source of career information. Your school counselor's office may also have career information available. The online version of the OOH [http://www.bls.gov/oco/] is a good starting point for Internet research.

	Marketing, Sales, and Service occupation:	Other occupation:
Qualifications/training		
Earnings		
Employment outlook		
Working conditions		
Typical duties		
Similar occupations		
Additional sources of information about this occupation		

Which of these two jobs would suit you better? Why?

_____

_____

ACTIVITY—MARKETING COMMUNICATIONS AND PROMOTION

In the late 1970s, advertising executive Donald Gunn developed a theory that almost all television advertisements fall into one of 12 basic categories, or "master formats." Go online or use your library's *Readers' Guide to Periodical Literature* to research Gunn's 12 categories. (***Hint:*** Use the keywords *Donald Gunn 12 advertisements* for an online search.) Then answer the following questions.

1. List three of Gunn's categories and identify a current television commercial that is an example of each.

_____

_____

_____

_____

_____

2. Think of a TV commercial you especially like. What makes this advertisement so effective?

_____

_____

_____

_____

_____

_____

3. Describe the kinds of services provided by advertising agencies. To find the information, try visiting the Web sites of two agencies (keyword search *advertising agency*). You may also use newspaper or magazine articles (try *Advertising Age* magazine or the business section of a newspaper).

_____

_____

_____

_____

_____

_____

ACTIVITY—E-COMMERCE

E-commerce is the buying and selling of goods and services online. If you have ever bought a book or music via the Internet, you've engaged in e-commerce. Employees involved in e-commerce perform a variety of functions. For example, they may design, develop, and maintain Web sites or use electronic tools to identify potential markets.

Successful e-businesses must have well-constructed, user-friendly Web sites. You can learn about good Web site design by visiting and studying existing successful e-commerce sites. (Examples include amazon.com, landsend.com, petopia.com, and garden.com). Also do some library/Internet research about basic Web design principles. (Use the *Readers' Guide to Periodical Literature* or search online using the keywords *web design*.) Then answer the following questions.

1. Of all the e-commerce sites you visited, which one was easiest to use? Explain.

_____

_____

_____

_____

_____

2. One key principle of Web site design is to avoid large graphics that take a long time to load onto the screen. Describe three other principles you should follow when designing an e-commerce Web site.

_____

_____

_____

_____

_____

3. What kinds of skills would you need to create a top-quality e-commerce site? How many of these skills do *you* have?

_____

_____

_____

_____

ACTIVITY—MARKETING INFORMATION MANAGEMENT AND RESEARCH

http://www.mybestsegments.com

The statistical characteristics of human populations are called **demographics**. Demographics include personal information such as age, gender, and income. When marketers know the demographic information of their target audience, their messages can be targeted more effectively. Marketing information resources company Claritas provides demographic information for any residential ZIP Code in the United States. Visit the My Best Segments Web site, then answer the following questions.

1. Enter the ZIP Code 40472 and read about the demographic characteristics of the people in that community. What types of businesses do you think would appeal to these people?

_____

_____

_____

_____

_____

2. Enter your own ZIP Code into the system. Does the demographic description seem accurate to you? Why or why not?

_____

_____

_____

_____

_____

3. Suppose you operate a ski equipment store. How could demographic information help you find the most likely customers?

_____

_____

_____

_____

_____

ACTIVITY—THE SEVEN FUNCTIONS OF MARKETING

Marketing activities can be organized into seven functions. Each function occurs every time a product or service is developed and sold. Businesses provide many of the marketing functions. Consumers often are responsible for one or more of the marketing functions when they make purchases.

The seven marketing functions are listed below. Use library/Internet resources to help you write each one next to its description.

☐ Product/service management
☐ Distribution
☐ Selling

☐ Marketing-information management
☐ Financing

☐ Promotion
☐ Pricing

	communicating directly with potential customers to evaluate and meet their needs
	securing funds needed for operations, budgeting for marketing activities, and arranging loans and payment plans to help customers purchase the business's products and services
	delivering information about products and services to potential customers to persuade them to buy
	developing, designing, maintaining, and improving products and services so they meet consumer needs
	determining the value of products and services and communicating that value to potential customers
	gathering and using market information to make business decisions and improve the marketing process
	selecting the processes that most effectively allow customers to find, acquire, and use the business's products and services

ACTIVITY—DISTRIBUTION AND LOGISTICS

You work as a shipping clerk for Altman Booksellers. As part of your job, you must fill out a packing slip for each order. You must also find the least expensive way to ship packages so customers receive them the second business day after they have been shipped. Today you are filling out a packing slip for the following order:

- ☐ *Customer:* Alan Smithee, 740 Elberon Avenue, Cincinnati, OH 45205 (same shipping and billing address; this is a residential address)
- ☐ *Purchase Order number:* 11540
- ☐ *Order number:* 540
- ☐ *Customer Account:* AS894
- ☐ *Items ordered:* 1 copy *Desktop Publishing Made Easy* ($32.95/each); 1 copy *99 Freelancing Tips* ($18.99/each); 2 copies *How to Work from Home* ($15.95/each)

A 6% sales tax is added to the subtotal of the order. You must complete the packing slip, then compare shipping costs for this item using FedEx, UPS, and the U.S. Postal Service. (Call each carrier or visit their Web sites.) The total weight of the package is three pounds. You will drop the package off at the nearest post office or FedEx/UPS station yourself as part of your daily rounds.

Altman Booksellers
4234 Pine Street
San Francisco, CA 94125

Order Date: Order Number:
Purchase Order: Customer Account:
Ship to: Bill to:

Quantity	Item	Item Price	Total
		Subtotal	
		Tax	
		Shipping	
		Order Total	

Thank you for your order!

ACTIVITY—MANAGEMENT AND ENTREPRENEURSHIP

People who own, operate, and take the risk of a business venture are called **entrepreneurs**. What kind of people go into business for themselves? Researchers have identified several characteristics that most successful entrepreneurs have. For example, entrepreneurs tend to be independent. They like making their own decisions.

What other personal traits and characteristics do you think you need to run your own business? Write your answers in the space below.

_____

_____

_____

_____

_____

Now that you have thought a bit about the characteristics of successful entrepreneurs, find out if *you* have what it takes to be one yourself. Do an online search using the keywords *entrepreneur test*, then take the quiz you find. Report your results in the space below.

If you do not have Internet access, tell if you think you have the traits you identified in the first question above.

_____

_____

_____

_____

_____

Based on this activity, do you think you would like to own and operate your own business? Would you be successful? Why or why not?

_____

_____

_____

_____

_____

_____

ACTIVITY—DESIGN A LOGO

Betsy McIntosh is the owner/operator of the Backporch Restaurant, a medium-size diner located at 130 Main Street in Berea, Kentucky. The Backporch Restaurant specializes in southern-style cooking, but Betsy updates traditional recipes with a healthy, fresh approach that has made her diner quite popular.

Betsy has come to your graphic design studio for some ideas for a new logo for the Backporch Restaurant. She wants to use this logo on menus, in advertisements, and even on the new Web site she plans to launch soon. In the space below, sketch out one or two ideas for a Backporch Restaurant logo. (You may also use graphing paper or a computer graphics program to create your design if you wish.) Feel free to research other restaurant logos, facts about Berea, Kentucky, or anything else you think would help you prepare an effective design.

EXPLORING A CAREER IN THE MARKETING, SALES & SERVICE CLUSTER

The O*NET program (http://online.onetcenter.org/) is the nation's primary source of occupational information. O*NET provides data on thousands of specific jobs, including typical tasks, knowledge/skills, work styles, and education required by each. Visit the O*NET site to complete this activity. (If you do not have Internet access, gather information from your library's print version of the *Occupational Outlook Handbook*.)

1. Click the Find Occupations link. In the Quick Search box, enter a job title from the Marketing, Sales & Service Career Cluster that interests you. View the Details report.

(*Note:* Sample occupations in this Career Cluster can be found at the www.careerclusters.org Web site or from your teacher.)

2. Use the information you find at O*NET to fill out the following chart for the job title you chose. List the top three characteristics of the items with an asterisk (*).

Tasks*	Tools & Technology*	Knowledge*	Skills*
Abilities*	Work Activities*	Work Context*	Interests*
Work Styles*	Work Values*	Work Needs*	Related Occupations
Education Required	Median Wages	Employment	Projected Growth

3. Would you be interested in this job? Why or why not?

_____

_____

_____

Passions
- ☐ Creating order
- ☐ Knowing the proper procedures and standards
- ☐ Valuing consistency

Attitude
- ☐ Organized
- ☐ Honest, dependable, and responsible

Talents
- ☐ High energy level
- ☐ Good with words
- ☐ Organizing and leading ability

Heart
- ☐ Likes to work with people
- ☐ Likes to coordinate projects

Some Career Areas to Consider
- ☐ Administrative assistant
- ☐ Human resources manager
- ☐ Accountant
- ☐ Business analyst
- ☐ Store manager

Employment Outlook
- ☐ Jobs in business management and administration are expected to grow through 2014, especially for people with college degrees.
- ☐ Employment opportunities in accounting and human resources are expected to grow faster than the average for all occupations.
- ☐ Positions in business analysis appear in the Bureau of Labor Statistics' list of "Hottest Jobs."

ACTIVITY—MANAGEMENT

Just about every type of business—from restaurants to hospitals to factories—employ managers. **Management** is getting work done through others. Pat Carrigan, a manager at a General Motors car parts plant, said, "I've never made a part in my life. . . . That's not my job. My job is to create an environment where people who do make them can make them right, can make them right the first time, can make them at a competitive cost, and can do so with some sense of responsibility and pride in what they're doing. I don't have to know how to make a part to do any of those things."

As Carrigan's words suggest, managers supervise other employees. In fact, unlike other employees, a manager's performance is often judged on how well *other* people do their jobs.

Large businesses often have several layers of management. First-line managers hold positions like office manager, shift supervisor, or production manager. These managers generally supervise employees who produce the company's goods or services. Middle managers hold positions like regional manager or department head. A regional sales manager, for example, might be responsible for several teams of sales representatives in the company's eastern region. A company's top manager might be called the chief executive officer (CEO) or chief operating officer (COO). The top manager is responsible for the overall operation of the company.

Writers in the field of management often classify a manager's job into four basic functions: planning, organizing, leading, and controlling.

- ☐ **Planning:** determining the organization's goals and ways to achieve these goals
- ☐ **Organizing:** deciding who will do what tasks and who will work for whom in the organization
- ☐ **Leading:** inspiring or motivating workers to work hard toward achieving the organization's goals
- ☐ **Controlling:** monitoring progress toward goal achievement and taking corrective action when progress is not being made

Directions: Suppose that your class decides to work for a day at your local park as a community service project. The tasks will include picking up trash, clearing overgrown trails, and planting trees. You have agreed to manage the project. Use the information from the article and your own experiences to answer the following questions.

1. **Specifying** What is your role as the project manager?

_____

_____

_____

_____

_____

2. **Planning** What details would you include in your plan for the day?

_____

_____

_____

_____

_____

3. **Organizing** How would you organize the class to accomplish the tasks?

_____

_____

_____

_____

_____

4. **Leading** What would you do to motivate your classmates to do their tasks well?

_____

_____

_____

_____

_____

5. **Controlling** The people clearing a trail have encountered a fallen tree across the trail. They have no saw to remove the tree, and they are standing around trying to decide what to do. What would you do to get them moving again toward achieving the group's goals?

_____

_____

_____

_____

_____

6. **Assessing** Based on the article and your answers to the questions above, what kinds of personal characteristics does a good project manager need? Which of these characteristics do _you_ have?

_____

_____

_____

_____

_____

ORGANIZING CAREER CHOICES

Directions: Choose one of the following occupations from the Business, Management & Administration Cluster: public relations manager, training and development specialist, bookkeeper, auditor, administrative assistant, or data entry specialist. Then use the following table to compare and contrast it with an occupation from another Career Cluster of your choice. Finally, tell which job would suit you best. Conduct library/Internet research to locate the necessary information.

Hint: The *Occupational Outlook Handbook* (OOH) is available in most public libraries and is a good source of career information. Your school counselor's office may also have career information available. The online version of the OOH [http://www.bls.gov/oco/] is a good starting point for Internet research.

	Business, Management & Administration occupation:	**Other occupation:**
Qualifications/training		
Earnings		
Employment outlook		
Working conditions		
Typical duties		
Similar occupations		
Additional sources of information about this occupation		

Which of these two jobs would suit you better? Why?

ACTIVITY—HUMAN RESOURCES

Many specialists in human resources recruit, interview, and hire employees to fill open positions. The best choice is the candidate whose strengths best match the requirements of the job. For example, a receptionist must make a good first impression on visitors. For this job, human resource specialists would look for someone who is outgoing and friendly. A bookkeeping job requires different strengths. Human resource specialists might look for someone who is good with details and has strong computer skills.

1. Select a job that interests you. Do library or online research to learn the qualifications for this job. Write five qualifications that you think are most important to be successful in this job.

_____

_____

_____

2. Read advertisements for jobs in a newspaper or online to see how they are structured. Then write an advertisement to recruit applicants for the job you selected.

_____

_____

_____

_____

_____

_____

_____

3. Write five interview questions to ask applicants for the job you advertised. Each question should target one of the key qualifications you identified in question 1.

_____

_____

_____

_____

_____

ACTIVITY—BUSINESS ETHICS

"Ethics" refers to the set of core values that help people determine right from wrong. However, many problems have no clearly "right" solution. You have to evaluate your options and make the best choice you can. To help evaluate your options, ask yourself these questions: Would I be acting honestly? Would I be comfortable with this choice? Would I be embarrassed if my friends and family knew my choice? Would this choice cause anyone harm? Think about what you would do in the following situation.

You are the manager of a small company that makes furniture. Over many years, your company has earned a reputation for using only the highest quality materials and workmanship. Business has been slow lately, and you worry that you may have to lay off some workers. Then a large chain of retail stores offers to carry your brand. To sell at the price the chain demands, however, you would have to lower your standards and use cheaper fabrics, woods, and stains.

1. Name two ways you might handle this situation.

_____

_____

_____

_____

2. What are the advantages and disadvantages of each option?

_____

_____

_____

_____

3. Which option would you choose? Why?

_____

_____

_____

_____

_____

_____

ACTIVITY—BUSINESS ANALYSIS

Like people, businesses seldom have all the money they want. They have to choose the best ways to use their limited resources. Budget analysts help companies make these difficult decisions. A budget analyst develops a **budget**—a formal plan for dividing up income among spending and saving options. The company then uses its money according to the budget. Later, the budget analyst reviews the results.

Create a budget for yourself for one week. Estimate the income you will have to spend, including income you expect to receive, next to its source. Use the blank spaces to list other income sources you might have. Then identify the things you expect to buy and estimate the amounts you expect to spend in each category. Use the blank spaces to list other expected purchases. Include the amount you expect to save. Add up the income and spending/saving columns. Are they equal? If not, adjust your expected purchases. You can't spend what you don't have!

BUDGET FOR THE WEEK OF:					
Income			**Spending and Saving**		
Source	**Expected Amount**	**Actual Amount**	**Purchases**	**Expected Amount**	**Actual Amount**
Allowance			School lunches		
Job			Snacks		
Cash gifts			Movies/videos		
			Music		
			Clothes		
			Savings		
TOTAL			**TOTAL**		

Throughout the week, keep track of all your income and purchases. Record the week's total for each item in the "Actual" column. Did you make the best choices for using your limited resources? If not, what would you do differently to use your money better?

_____

_____

_____

_____

ACTIVITY—MARKETING

Marketing managers develop a strategy to sell the company's products. A key part of any marketing strategy is brand image. A **brand** is a name, symbol, or design that helps set a product apart from its competitors. For example, Nike is a well-known brand name of athletic shoes and clothing. The Nike swoosh symbol is a key part of the Nike brand. When consumers see the swoosh, they quickly associate the product with Nike.

Marketing managers work with people in advertising to create an image for their brand. The image is designed to attract the type of customer who might be most interested in their product. The image might include a slogan used over and over in advertising. Nike, for example, often used the phrase "Just do it!" as part of its brand image.

1. Go to a store and look at a similar product from two different companies—for example, different brands of shampoo. Note the two brand names. On a separate sheet of paper, or in a new computer file, draw or describe the symbols or designs each company used on the packaging to set its product apart.

2. View an advertisement on television, or read one online or in a magazine. How would you describe the brand image the ad is creating? How does the ad make the product seem fun? Useful? Fashionable?

_____

_____

_____

3. Think of the product you identified in question 2. What type of customer do you think the ad is trying to attract? For example, is it directed at someone who wants a good value? Someone who is health-conscious? Identify two things in the ad to explain your answer.

_____

_____

_____

_____

4. Based on this activity, do you think you would like to work in marketing? Why or why not?

_____

_____

_____

ACTIVITY—BUSINESS FINANCIAL MANAGEMENT AND ACCOUNTING

You work as a payroll clerk for Music Planet. An important part of your job is to calculate each employee's pay for the week. The law requires employers to deduct, or subtract, several types of taxes from each employee's pay and send the money to the government. **Gross pay** is the amount earned before deductions are subtracted. **Net pay** is the amount the employee receives after deductions are subtracted. Net pay is the amount the employee actually receives in the paycheck.

You are preparing a paycheck for Jason Katz. Jason's makes $9.50 per hour. He worked 40 hours this week. The government requires these percentages to be deducted from gross pay: federal income tax: 15%; Social Security tax, 6%; Medicare tax: 1%; state tax, 0.5%. Use these figures to calculate Jason's net pay for his paycheck stub below. If you have access to spreadsheet software, create formulas in a spreadsheet to make the calculations for you.

Music Planet 522 Walnut Street Anytown, ST 12345		Check No. **26775**
Employee: Jason Katz 65 Chase Street Anytown, ST 12345	Social Security Number: 222-33-4444	Pay period ending: 11/10/--
Earnings	**Deductions**	
Hours worked: _____	Federal Income Tax: _____	Gross Pay: _____
Hourly rate: _____	Social Security Tax: _____	Total Deductions: _____
Gross Pay: _____	Medicare Tax: _____	
	State Tax: _____	Net Pay: _____
	Total Deductions: _____	

When Jason cashes his check, how much money will he have in his pocket?

_____

Based on this activity, what kinds of personal characteristics does a good payroll clerk need? Which of these characteristics do *you* have?

_____

_____

_____

ACTIVITY—Administration and Information Support

Have you ever been unhappy with a product? Did you call or go to the store's customer service desk to complain? You were probably not in a good mood, so you may not have been especially pleasant with the customer service representative.

Now put yourself in the representative's shoes. Your job is to answer questions from customers and resolve their problems. Not every customer contacts you to complain. In fact, most questions are routine, such as asking the status of an order. No matter why customers call, your manager expects you to respond in a friendly, helpful manner. You want to please the customers so they will continue to do business with your company.

1. Think about a situation in which you were unhappy with a product. Perhaps the product did not work or it was not as it appeared in the catalog. In the space below, compose an email to the company's customer service representative. Describe the problem in as much detail as you can. (Use library/Internet resources to find examples of complaint letters before you begin writing— use the keywords *complaint letter* in your search.)

_____

_____

_____

_____

_____

_____

_____

2. Now take the role of the customer service representative who receives the email you wrote in question 1. Write a response to the complaint. In the response, offer a solution. Be friendly and positive. Remember—You want to keep the customer's business.

_____

_____

_____

_____

_____

_____

ACTIVITY—NAME THAT JOB

Several jobs in the Business, Management, and Administration Cluster appear in the list below. The following statements give clues to the employee's job. Based on the job titles and what you have learned in this chapter, identify the job each employee holds. If you are unsure, read the job descriptions in *The Occupational Outlook Handbook* in the library or at O*NET online (http://online.onetcenter.org).

budget analyst

chief executive officer

customer service representative

marketing manager

payroll clerk

regional sales manager

shift supervisor

training and development specialist

1. I am teaching a class on time management to help employees work more efficiently.

2. If we save 5 percent of our income this year, we can use the money to open a new store next year.

3. I'm sorry that you are having trouble with our product. I will look into the problem and get back to you.

4. After you turn in your time sheet, I will process your earnings and deductions and issue your check.

5. I coordinate the activities of all our sales representatives in the western states.

6. The workers I direct produce the company's best line of designer clothing.

7. I think the new marketing strategy I've developed will increase our profits this year.

8. I am responsible for the company's overall performance. The buck stops here.

EXPLORING A CAREER IN THE BUSINESS, MANAGEMENT, & ADMINISTRATION CLUSTER

The O*NET program (http://online.onetcenter.org/) is the nation's primary source of occupational information. O*NET provides data on thousands of specific jobs, including typical tasks, knowledge/skills, work styles, and education required by each. Visit the O*NET site to complete this activity. (If you do not have Internet access, gather information from your library's print version of the *Occupational Outlook Handbook*.)

1. Click the Find Occupations link. In the Quick Search box, enter a job title from the Business, Management & Administration Career Cluster that interests you. View the Details report.

(*Note:* Sample occupations in this Career Cluster can be found at the www.careerclusters.org Web site or from your teacher.)

2. Use the information you find at O*NET to fill out the following chart for the job title you chose. List the top three characteristics of the items with an asterisk (*).

Tasks*	Tools & Technology*	Knowledge*	Skills*
Abilities*	Work Activities*	Work Context*	Interests*
Work Styles*	Work Values*	Work Needs*	Related Occupations
Education Required	Median Wages	Employment	Projected Growth

3. Would you be interested in this job? Why or why not?

_____

_____

Passions
- ☐ Planning and organizing
- ☐ Meeting new people
- ☐ Influencing others' decisions

Attitude
- ☐ Sociable
- ☐ Dependable

Talents
- ☐ Ability to work with other people
- ☐ Outgoing personality
- ☐ Communication skills

Heart
- ☐ Likes detailed projects
- ☐ Likes to travel

Some Career Areas to Consider
- ☐ Restaurant server
- ☐ Interpreter
- ☐ Chef
- ☐ Resort instructor
- ☐ Hotel manager

Employment Outlook
- ☐ Travel and tourism is one of the largest and fastest-growing industries in the world.
- ☐ Each year, travel and tourism employers create 12.5 million new jobs. This Cluster tends to promote from within and to employ a large number of young managers.

ACTIVITY—TRAVEL AND TOURISM

One of the hottest trends in the hospitality field is **ecotourism**. Ecotourism appeals to travelers who want to protect the environment and support and respect the cultures of indigenous (native) people. As an ecotour guide, you might work for a South American tourism company, leading vacationers through the rain forests of Brazil or among the native peoples of the Andes Mountains. Or you could join an organization like the International Ecotourism Society, helping to educate tourism professionals about ecotourism.

As ecotourism has grown, however, ecotourism providers must keep a number of ethical questions in mind. For example, tourists must be careful not to leave trash behind at campsites, or disturb the native foliage. Fishing from a gasoline-powered boat might be considered unethical by some ecotourists, but paddling across a lake in a wooden canoe to snorkel might be acceptable. Local people may not appreciate being "observed" by tourists, who may unintentionally drive off the wildlife the native people need to survive.

Emily Coehlo has worked in ecotourism for ten years. She answers some questions about her work:

What kind of training do you need to work in ecotourism?

Travel experience is a huge advantage. Lots of outdoor experience is helpful, too. You really need to love nature and wildlife. A college degree in something like wildlife biology is useful. Having contacts in the industry can help, too.

What kinds of things do you do on the job?

Well, now I'm working in sales, so I spend most of time helping customers on the phone. I explain our trips to them, answer their questions . . . basically, I work with our customers to make sure their trip is exactly what they want. I also send a lot of emails to suppliers all around the world.

What about when you worked as a guide?

When I worked as a guide, my job was to show off the sights and explain their cultural, historical, and environmental importance. I had to know where to go, how to get there, and where to stay. Of course, there were challenges too. Weather and wildlife could often be a problem. Sometimes our treks took us to some dangerous places—mountains, rapids, deserts. I had to listen to the travelers' complaints and fix their problems as best I could.

What are some things you like the most about working in ecotourism?

Travel. The chance to help someone have a once-in-a-lifetime experience. A relaxed and fun but professional work environment. Independence.

Directions: Use the information from the article and your own experiences to answer the following questions.

1. **Defining** What is ecotourism?

_____

_____

_____

_____

2. **Identifying** According to Emily Coehlo, what kind of background is helpful for someone interested in a career in ecotourism?

_____

_____

_____

_____

_____

3. **Stating** Of all the "wild" places in the world, which would you most like to visit? Why?

_____

_____

_____

_____

4. **Problem-Solving** Suppose you are working as an ecoguide. One of the tourists in your party is a farmer, and he asks if it would be OK if he gave some advice to the native people in the area about how to improve their farming techniques. What would you answer? Why?

_____

_____

_____

_____

_____

5. **Comparing and Contrasting** How might visiting the Serengeti plains in Africa or the Australian outback be different from visiting a large city like Paris or Tokyo? How might it be the same?

_____

_____

_____

_____

_____

6. **Assessing** Based on the article, what kinds of personal characteristics does a good ecotourism provider need? How many of these characteristics do _you_ have?

_____

_____

_____

_____

_____

ORGANIZING CAREER CHOICES

Directions: Choose one of the following occupations from the Hospitality & Tourism Cluster: travel agent, zookeeper, reservations supervisor, or caterer. Then use the following table to compare and contrast it with an occupation from another Career Cluster of your choice. Finally, tell which job would suit you best. Conduct library/Internet research to locate the necessary information.

Hint: The *Occupational Outlook Handbook* (OOH) is available in most public libraries and is a good source of career information. Your school counselor's office may also have career information available. The online version of the OOH [http://www.bls.gov/oco/] is a good starting point for Internet research.

	Hospitality & Tourism occupation:	**Other occupation:**
Qualifications/training		
Earnings		
Employment outlook		
Working conditions		
Typical duties		
Similar occupations		
Additional sources of information about this occupation		

Which of these two jobs would suit you better? Why?

_____

_____

ACTIVITY—RECREATIONS, AMUSEMENTS, AND ATTRACTIONS

http://www.bumbershoot.org

The Seattle Music and Arts Festival, better known as Bumbershoot, has brought an amazing and diverse collection of music, art, and entertainment to the Pacific Northwest since 1971. Visit the event's Web site—or find some articles about the event in the library—to learn more.

1. Use a dictionary to find out what the word Bumbershoot means. Why do you think it was chosen as the name of this festival?

_____

_____

_____

_____

_____

2. Name some performers who have appeared at this festival. What does that tell you about the kind of audience that attends this event?

_____

_____

_____

_____

_____

_____

3. Suppose you were organizing a festival like Bumbershoot. Name three entertainers you would get for your festival. What kind of audience do you think those entertainers would attract?

_____

_____

_____

_____

_____

_____

_____

ACTIVITY—LODGING

A **concierge** is a hotel employee who helps guests perform personal chores such as making restaurant reservations, finding tickets to concerts or sporting events, and even shopping for gifts. Many expensive hotels promote the ability of their concierge staff to "do the impossible," promising to fulfill any unusual request a guest may have.

Concierges must always be calm and professional, no matter how outrageous a guest's request. They must keep up to date with the very best restaurants, stores, clubs, and theaters in town in order to direct guests effectively. They must also maintain a large network of friends and acquaintances to ensure that guests' demands are met.

1. You work as a concierge for a hotel in your community. A guest has asked you to make dinner reservations for her at "the best restaurant around." She also wants you to give her advice on a "fun place to visit" tomorrow morning. Give your recommendations in the space below.

_____

_____

_____

_____

_____

_____

_____

_____

_____

2. A guest has asked you to arrange a horse-drawn carriage ride for him and his children. How would you fill this request? Do any local businesses offer carriage rides? (Check through the phone book.) Do you have any friends or family members who could help? On a separate sheet of paper, explain how you would go about meeting this guest's request.

3. Do you think you would make a good concierge? Why or why not?

_____

_____

_____

_____

_____

ACTIVITY—RESTAURANT AND FOOD/BEVERAGE SERVICES

A **food writer** (sometimes called restaurant critic or food columnist) is someone who has a meal at a restaurant and writes about his or her experiences. In this exercise, you're going to take on the role of a food writer.

First, do some library/Internet research about how to be a food writer. Find some restaurant reviews online or in newspapers or magazines. Notice how critics write about meals. They describe what the food looked like, how it smelled, and how it tasted. They describe the restaurant and comment on the service they received. They also list prices and tell if they think the item is a good value.

After you have read some restaurant reviews and learned a bit more about being a food writer, you're ready to write your review. In the space below, write a review of a recent meal you ate in your school lunchroom. Be sure to detail all aspects of your dining experience.

_____

_____

_____

_____

_____

_____

_____

_____

_____

_____

_____

_____

_____

_____

_____

_____

_____

ACTIVITY— RECREATIONS, AMUSEMENTS, AND ATTRACTIONS

The popularity of the Women's National Basketball Association (WNBA) is not yet as great as the National Basketball Association (NBA). But the WNBA gets plenty of publicity on television and in the newspapers. WNBA fans are loyal and excited about the future of the league. Visit the WNBA Web site (www.wnba.com) and use library/Internet research (keywords *WNBA* or *women's basketball*) to help you answer the following questions.

1. Write the first three words that come to mind when you think of the WNBA. Then write the first three words that come to mind when you think of the NBA.

_____

_____

_____

2. The WNBA has used slogans such as "Join In" and "We Got Next" to symbolize opportunities for girls and women to develop an interest and talent in sports. Describe one more strategy you might use to promote the WNBA to girls.

_____

_____

_____

3. Suppose the WNBA wanted to attract more boys as fans. Describe a strategy you might use to promote the WNBA to boys.

_____

_____

_____

4. Do you think the WNBA will exist ten years from now? Explain your answer.

_____

_____

_____

5. Are you a fan of the WNBA? Why or why not?

_____

_____

_____

ACTIVITY—TRAVEL AND TOURISM

Tourism is a major source of income for many states. All 50 states have a state-level tourism organization, usually referred to as the Department of Tourism. A tourism organization's goal is to build an image of the state as a place people want to visit. Visit your state's tourism Web site or use library resources to answer these questions.

1. Name at least three activities and locations promoted by your state's Department of Tourism. How many of these have you visited?

_____

_____

_____

_____

2. Name one place in your state—or even your local community—that you enjoy visiting but that is not mentioned on your state's tourism Web site or in your state's tourism literature.

_____

_____

_____

_____

3. On a separate sheet of paper—or in a computer graphics program—prepare a flyer or brochure promoting the place you identified in question 2. Do some library/Internet research about the attraction you are going to write about. Think about why you like this place and why someone else might like it, too.

Here are some things to remember about your brochure:

- A brochure is not an in-depth report. You don't have to tell everything about the attraction. Choose two or three main points to emphasize.
- You can use a bulleted list (like this one) to provide information about a few other points.
- You must also decide the best way to present your information. Will you include mostly text; a mixture of text and art; lists, charts, maps?

- Things to consider for your brochure include
  o Main heading or title that creates reader interest
  o Name, address, phone number of the attraction
  o Short, easy-to-read text blocks
  o A map
  o A description of things to do at the attraction

ACTIVITY—NOW WE'RE COOKING!

Do you love to cook? Have people told you that you could be a chef or run your own diner? Let's see if you are ready. Take this little quiz to find out. (Your teacher has the correct answers to this quiz.)

1. You have decided to make a western omelet for breakfast. What kind of meat goes into a traditional western omelet?

A ham
B chicken
C beef
D turkey

2. You are making macaroni and cheese. What ingredient should you add to make sure it is extra creamy?

A eggs
B oil
C milk
D yogurt

3. What is hoppin' john?

A a type of hard-shelled clam
B a small, fried cornmeal dumpling
C a salad dressing made of oil and vinegar
D a dish of black-eyed peas and salt pork

4. If a recipe tells you to poach a food, what should you do?

A wrap it in foil and bake it
B add an egg to it
C cook it in a simmering liquid
D pop it in the refrigerator for an hour

5. If you are making *roux*, you are probably making

A bread.
B a sauce.
C pie.
D ice cream.

6. Which term describes pasta that is cooked enough to eat but is not overdone?

A foie gras
B a la mode
C al denté
D au gratin

7. In the space below, tell about a time you made a recipe at home. What was it? How did it turn out?

_____

_____

_____

_____

8. Based on how well you did on this quiz, do you think you would like to work as a cook? Why or why not?

_____

_____

_____

_____

ACTIVITY—LODGING

A clean room is one of the most important reasons why a guest chooses one motel or hotel over another. The housekeeping crew is responsible for the daily cleaning of guest rooms.

Would the bedrooms and bathrooms where you live pass inspection by a professional motel/hotel housekeeper? Use the checklist below to inspect a bedroom and a bathroom in your home.

Guest Room Housekeeping Checklist	
BEDROOM	☐ Floors vacuumed/cleaned ☐ Walls and ceilings cleaned ☐ Outside windows washed ☐ Inside windows washed ☐ Window sills cleaned ☐ Curtains/shades cleaned ☐ Clean/fresh linens ☐ Beds made ☐ Furniture dusted ☐ Wastebaskets emptied ☐ Mirrors clean ☐ Lampshades dusted ☐ Burned out light bulbs replaced ☐ Shelves dusted ☐ Cobwebs removed
BATHROOM	☐ Tub/shower cleaned and disinfected ☐ Tiles scrubbed ☐ Toilet cleaned and disinfected ☐ Sink cleaned and disinfected ☐ Water taps polished ☐ Inside of shower curtain clean ☐ Shelves wiped clean ☐ Mirrors clean ☐ Floor washed ☐ Fresh towels available ☐ Soap and shampoo available ☐ Facial and toilet tissue available

What kinds of personal characteristics does a good housekeeping employee need? How many of these characteristics do *you* have?

_____

_____

_____

_____

EXPLORING A CAREER IN THE HOSPITALITY & TOURISM CLUSTER

The O*NET program (http://online.onetcenter.org/) is the nation's primary source of occupational information. O*NET provides data on thousands of specific jobs, including typical tasks, knowledge/skills, work styles, and education required by each. Visit the O*NET site to complete this activity. (If you do not have Internet access, gather information from your library's print version of the *Occupational Outlook Handbook*.)

1. Click the Find Occupations link. In the Quick Search box, enter a job title from the Hospitality & Tourism Career Cluster that interests you. View the Details report.

(*Note:* Sample occupations in this Career Cluster can be found at the www.careerclusters.org Web site or from your teacher.)

2. Use the information you find at O*NET to fill out the following chart for the job title you chose. List the top three characteristics of the items with an asterisk (*).

Tasks*	Tools & Technology*	Knowledge*	Skills*
Abilities*	Work Activities*	Work Context*	Interests*
Work Styles*	Work Values*	Work Needs*	Related Occupations
Education Required	Median Wages	Employment	Projected Growth

3. Would you be interested in this job? Why or why not?

_____

_____

_____

Passions

☐ Finding solutions to problems

☐ Working with math

☐ Respecting ethics

Attitude

☐ Detail-oriented

☐ Logical thinker

Talents

☐ Record keeping skills

☐ Ability to handle money with accuracy

☐ Calm under pressure

Heart

☐ Prefers working inside

☐ Is admired by others

Some Career Areas to Consider

☐ Bank teller

☐ Stockbroker

☐ Financial planner

☐ Debt counselor

☐ Insurance appraiser

Employment Outlook

☐ Increases in global investing are expected to fuel job growth in the investment industry by 15.5 percent through the year 2012.

☐ Accounting jobs are expected to experience average growth.

☐ Jobs for tellers will decline, while growth is expected for loan officers and jobs in customer service and financial services.

ACTIVITY—FINANCIAL AND INVESTMENT PLANNING

Most likely, you will deposit your first savings in a bank account. The bank will pay you **interest**—a percentage of your account balance. As your savings grow, you will probably want to invest in stocks and bonds. These investments can help your money grow faster than it can in a bank account. When your investments grow large enough, you may want the services of a certified financial planner.

When you buy **stock**, you are investing in a corporation. As a stockholder, you would actually be a part owner of the corporation. You might also invest in bonds. **Bonds** are loans to corporations or governments. The organization is required to repay the amount invested in its bonds, with interest, at a stated time. Stocks and bonds help your money grow by providing a **return**, or percentage of the amount invested. But which stocks and bonds should you buy? A financial planner can help you answer this question.

Financial planners help people plan how to invest their money to achieve their goals, such as money for a college education or a secure retirement. Your financial planner will meet with you to determine your financial needs and goals. The planner will then suggest a set of investments in stocks and bonds that will help meet your goals.

This process is more complex than it first appears. Investing is risky. Unlike interest on a bank account, the return on your investment is not guaranteed. The prices of stocks and bonds go up and down. If you buy a stock at a high price and sell it at a lower price, you will lose money. If the company goes bankrupt, you could lose your entire investment. However, the amount of risk varies. The prices of some stocks rise and fall less than others. Bonds tend to be less risky because their prices remain more stable.

A basic principle of investing is that *the greater the potential return, the greater the risk.* If an investment is especially risky, then the potential return must be high enough to be worth taking the risk. Some people can tolerate more risk than others. To reduce the risk, planners advise investors to **diversify**, or put money into a wide variety of investments. As the famous investment manager Peter Lynch put it, "I think the secret is if you have a lot of stocks, some will do mediocre, some will do okay, and if one or two of 'em go up big time, you will produce a fabulous result." Your financial planner will help you find a mix of investments that will help your money grow at a reasonable rate while keeping the risk within your comfort zone.

Directions: Use the information from the article and your own experiences to answer the following questions.

1. **Contrasting** Why are investments in stocks and bonds riskier than saving money at a bank?

_____

_____

_____

_____

_____

2. **Making Decisions** After you start investing in stocks and bonds, do you think you will continue to keep some money in a bank account? Why or why not?

_____

_____

_____

_____

_____

3. **Making Connections** How would you describe your tolerance for risk? Do you enjoy taking risks or do you prefer to avoid risk?

_____

_____

_____

_____

_____

4. **Explaining** How can a certified financial planner help you keep the investment risk to a level that is comfortable for you?

_____

_____

_____

_____

_____

5. **Drawing Conclusions** Suppose you read about a stock that went up a whopping 20% last year. What can you conclude about the risk level of this stock? Would you buy the stock? Why or why not?

_____

_____

_____

_____

_____

6. **Assessing** Based on the article, what kinds of personal characteristics does a good financial planner need? Which of these characteristics do *you* have?

_____

_____

_____

_____

_____

ORGANIZING CAREER CHOICES

Directions: Choose one of the following occupations from the Finance Cluster: tax preparer, economist, loan officer, or insurance sales agent. Then use the following table to compare and contrast it with an occupation from another Career Cluster of your choice. Finally, tell which job would suit you best. Conduct library/Internet research to locate the necessary information.

Hint: The *Occupational Outlook Handbook* (OOH) is available in most public libraries and is a good source of career information. Your school counselor's office may also have career information available. The online version of the OOH [http://www.bls.gov/oco/] is a good starting point for Internet research.

	Finance occupation:	**Other occupation:**
Qualifications/training		
Earnings		
Employment outlook		
Working conditions		
Typical duties		
Similar occupations		
Additional sources of information about this occupation		

Which of these two jobs would suit you better? Why?

_____

_____

ACTIVITY—BANKING AND RELATED SERVICES

Unfortunately, too many Americans have spent themselves into debt trouble. They use their credit cards freely, thinking they will pay for these purchases later. Soon, the credit card balances grow so large that paying them off seems hopeless. Many people in this situation seek help from a debt counselor.

Debt counselors give advice on how to manage money effectively. They teach clients how to make and follow a budget. They might advise clients to discard their credit cards and live on cash to avoid future trouble. In cases of severe debt, counselors develop a payment plan. Clients agree to make a monthly deposit with the counseling agency, which distributes the money to the clients' creditors. Often counselors can negotiate with the credit card companies for lower interest rates for clients who agree to enroll in the payment plan.

> Suppose you ran up a balance of $1,000 on your Visa card. The interest rate is 12%. The minimum required payment is $15. You want to pay off the debt before you make any more purchases with the card. Use library resources or an online debt reduction calculator (search using keywords *debt reduction calculator*) to answer the questions.

1. If you make payments of $30 a month, how long will it take to pay off the Visa debt mentioned above? How much interest will you pay?

2. Suppose the bank raises the interest rate to 15%. If you pay $30 a month, how long will it take to pay off the debt at this new rate? What is the dollar amount of the interest you will pay?

3. How does an increase in the interest rate affect your monthly payment?

4. Suppose you decide to make just the minimum required payment of $15 each month. At 12%, how long will it take to pay off the debt? How much interest will you pay?

5. Draw one conclusion about the effect of making just the minimum monthly payments.

42   Finance

ACTIVITY—INSURANCE SERVICES

If you are a teenage boy, you will probably pay more for car insurance than a girl your age. Why? Insurance actuaries study statistics from the past to see how losses occurred. From this information, they can predict that losses will occur more often in some situations than in others. The company then charges higher rates to people in high-risk groups. For example, statistics show that teenage boys have more car accidents than teenage girls. Here are other characteristics that will affect the cost of your car insurance:

- ☐ age and gender
- ☐ single or married
- ☐ where you live

- ☐ driving record
- ☐ grades in school
- ☐ type of car you drive

1. Would you expect a 30-year-old driver to pay more or less for car insurance than you will when you first begin to drive? Why?

_____

_____

_____

2. Do you think more accidents occur in a big city or a small town? How would this affect the rates drivers pay in these areas?

_____

_____

_____

3. Why would it cost more to insure an expensive sports car than an economy car?

_____

_____

_____

4. Name two things you can you do to reduce the cost of your car insurance.

_____

_____

_____

_____

ACTIVITY—BUSINESS FINANCIAL MANAGEMENT

You are the financial analyst for a real estate company that sells homes. Your boss wants to know if this is a good time to hire more sales agents. Your job is to analyze economic data to help make this decision. The table below shows data for your area. Analyze the information by looking for trends and interpreting their meaning.

	2005	2006	2007
Growth in number of homes sold	–2%	3%	6%
Average price of homes sold	$100,000	$120,000	$180,000
Average days on market before homes sell	90	60	30
Overall growth of local economy	2%	3%	5%

1. What trend do you see in the number of homes sold? Is this trend good or bad for your business? Why?

_____

_____

_____

_____

2. The trend for average days on the market is going down. Is this a good sign or bad sign for your business? Why?

_____

_____

_____

_____

3. Would you recommend hiring more sales agents? Why or why not?

_____

_____

_____

_____

ACTIVITY—TYPES OF INSURANCE

The purpose of insurance is to limit your financial loss if disaster strikes. For example, if a storm damages your house, your homeowner's insurance will help pay for repairs. Insurance companies offer a variety of plans to cover different kinds of unfortunate events. Some common types of insurance are:

☐ automobile insurance   ☐ life insurance
☐ disability insurance   ☐ malpractice insurance
☐ health insurance   ☐ renter's insurance
☐ homeowner's insurance   ☐ worker's compensation insurance

1. Describe three different "disasters" that could happen in your life.

_____

_____

_____

_____

2. Do library or online research to learn about the kinds of losses covered by each insurance in the list above. Which type would you need for the disasters you described in question 1?

_____

_____

_____

_____

3. Which types of insurance will you need when you finish school, take your first full-time job, and begin living in your own apartment? Explain why.

_____

_____

_____

_____

ACTIVITY—THREE C'S OF CREDIT

You are a loan officer at a bank. Your job is to evaluate loan applications, ask the applicants questions, and decide whether to approve the loans. When you recommend loaning money to someone, you want to be confident the person will repay the loan. You base your judgment on the "three C's of credit":

☐ **Character:** Do the applicants take their financial obligations seriously? Are they dependable?

☐ **Capacity:** Do the applicants have the financial capacity (ability) to repay? Do they make enough money? Do they already have more debt than they can handle?

☐ **Capital:** Do the applicants have investments or own valuable property that could be turned into cash, if needed, to repay the loan?

1. Write three questions you would ask to help evaluate an applicant's "character."

_____

_____

_____

2. What types of financial information would you need to judge "capacity"?

_____

_____

3. Suppose an applicant told you that she has three credit cards. Is this a good sign or a red flag? Explain.

_____

_____

_____

4. Based on this activity, do you think you would like to work as a loan officer? Explain.

_____

_____

_____

_____

ACTIVITY—THE LANGUAGE OF INVESTING

Does a career in investments appeal to you? Perhaps you would like to be a stockbroker, so that you could buy and sell stocks for your clients. Or maybe you would enjoy working as an investment advisor or investment analyst. To help you decide, become familiar with the language of investing. Based on what you learned in this section, plus some library or Internet research, match the investment terms below to their meanings.

☐ bond
☐ diversify
☐ dividend
☐ load
☐ mutual fund

☐ return
☐ risk
☐ stock
☐ stock exchange
☐ ticker symbol

Term	Meaning
1.	the chance that an investment will decrease in value
2.	put money into a variety of investments to reduce overall risk
3.	an investment that makes the investor a part owner of the corporation
4.	the amount or percentage earned on an investment
5.	a portion of a corporation's profits paid to the stockholders
6.	an investment that requires the corporation to repay the amount invested, with interest, at a stated time
7.	a group of investments owned by many investors
8.	a place, either physical or electronic, where investors buy and sell stocks
9.	a sales fee investors pay when they buy some types of mutual funds
10	an abbreviation made up of several letters that identifies a particular stock or mutual fund

ACTIVITY—FINANCIAL ETHICS

Money often plays a role in ethical issues. Consumers want low prices. Companies try to cut costs so they can offer the low prices consumers want. Companies also want to make a profit for their owners. Without profit, they would go out of business. Sometimes conflicting financial goals can lead to ethical dilemmas. As you evaluate the following situations, ask yourself questions like these: Who could be helped? Who could be hurt? Am I comfortable with these actions?

1. You are a financial planner. Like many people in your line of work, you make most of your money from commissions on the investment products you sell. The amount of the commission varies. You earn more from selling some investments than others. Today, you are helping a client decide which investment to buy. Several good investments will fit the client's financial plan, including a new one that the company wants to promote. The company will pay you an especially high commission to encourage you to sell this investment. The cost to the client will be a bit higher than for the other options, but it is a promising investment. Will you recommend the new investment to your client? Why or why not?

_____

_____

_____

_____

2. You work at a health insurance company. To make a profit, your company must take in more money in premiums than it pays out in claims. Your company follows several policies to try to hold down the cost of claims. Since obese people tend to have more health problems, the company will not offer insurance to anyone who is more than 20 pounds overweight. People with a serious illness, such as cancer, require a lot of expensive care. When insured people become seriously ill, the company raises their premiums each year to help cover the costs. Some of these people eventually drop the insurance because they can no longer afford it, further reducing costs. By saving money in these ways, the company can offer insurance to most people at reasonable rates. Do you agree with these policies? Why or why not?

_____

_____

_____

_____

EXPLORING A CAREER IN THE FINANCE CLUSTER

The O*NET program (http://online.onetcenter.org/) is the nation's primary source of occupational information. O*NET provides data on thousands of specific jobs, including typical tasks, knowledge/skills, work styles, and education required by each. Visit the O*NET site to complete this activity. (If you do not have Internet access, gather information from your library's print version of the *Occupational Outlook Handbook*.)

1. Click the Find Occupations link. In the Quick Search box, enter a job title from the Finance Career Cluster that interests you. View the Details report.

(*Note:* Sample occupations in this Career Cluster can be found at the www.careerclusters.org Web site or from your teacher.)

2. Use the information you find at O*NET to fill out the following chart for the job title you chose. List the top three characteristics of the items with an asterisk (*).

Tasks*	Tools & Technology*	Knowledge*	Skills*
Abilities*	Work Activities*	Work Context*	Interests*
Work Styles*	Work Values*	Work Needs*	Related Occupations
Education Required	Median Wages	Employment	Projected Growth

3. Would you be interested in this job? Why or why not?

_____

_____

_____

Passions
- ☐ Solving problems
- ☐ Working with details
- ☐ Helping people

Attitude
- ☐ Confident
- ☐ Analytical

Talents
- ☐ Ability to relate to many types of people
- ☐ Ability to communicate well by writing and speaking
- ☐ Ability to make quick decisions

Heart
- ☐ Is trustworthy
- ☐ Is caring

Some Career Areas to Consider
- ☐ Firefighter
- ☐ Lawyer
- ☐ Parole officer
- ☐ Police dispatcher
- ☐ Security guard

Employment Outlook
- ☐ Job opportunities will be good in this Career Cluster due to a growing desire for corporate, industrial, and homeland security. Public concern about crime should contribute to the increasing demand.
- ☐ Growth should be greater than average for legal assistants, paralegals, and workers in correction services.

ACTIVITY—LAW ENFORCEMENT SERVICES

Hogan's Alley is probably the most dangerous town in America. There's only one bank, but it's robbed every week. Gang members walk the streets freely. Drug dealers are everywhere. And just about every car in town has been stolen at one time or another.

And the FBI wouldn't want it any other way.

Hogan's Alley was created in 1987 to help the Federal Bureau of Investigation (FBI) train new agents. The make-believe town is located on the grounds of the FBI Training Academy in Quantico, Virginia. It was built by top Hollywood set designers and features a bank, a post office, a hotel, houses, and businesses. Hogan's Alley looks so real that visitors have been known to line up for tickets at the town's Biograph Theater or to try to get a meal at the Dogwood Inn Restaurant!

New agents are very busy patrolling Hogan's Alley. They learn the most up-to-date investigative techniques, firearms skills, and defensive techniques. They learn how to handle evidence at crime scenes and how to make arrests. They even interview witnesses and crime victims and get into gunfights with criminals (all of whom are played by local actors).

Occasionally, the new recruits get a surprise. FBI instructors sometimes ask the actor-criminals to resist arrest or even throw a punch at an agent—just like in real life. Sometimes witnesses don't want to tell everything they know. This helps the new agents practice the skills they will need when they leave Hogan's Alley and get to work in communities all over America.

FBI agents have many different responsibilities: community outreach, crime prevention, even completing paperwork related to investigations. With such a wide variety of duties, every day on the job is different. Thanks to the training they receive at Hogan's Alley, they are well equipped to protect us—and themselves.

Directions: Use the information from the article and your own experiences to answer the following questions.

1. **Identifying** What is Hogan's Alley? Where is it located?

_____

_____

_____

_____

_____

2. **Listing** What are some things new FBI agents learn at Hogan's Alley?

_____

_____

_____

_____

_____

3. **Making Inferences** Why do you think the FBI went to the time and expense to create a make-believe town in which to train new agents?

_____

_____

_____

_____

_____

4. **Differentiating** Identify two ways the training that agents receive at Hogan's Alley is probably different from the training they might receive in a classroom. Which do you think is more valuable? Why?

_____

_____

_____

_____

5. **Making Connections** Have you ever participated in a classroom simulation in which you took on the role of someone from history, or someone working in a particular profession? Briefly describe the simulation. Do you think you learned more from role-playing the situation than you would have learned simply from reading about it?

_____

_____

_____

_____

6. **Assessing** Based on the article, what kinds of personal characteristics does a good FBI agent need? How many of these characteristics do _you_ have?

_____

_____

_____

_____

ORGANIZING CAREER CHOICES

Directions: Choose one of the following occupations from the Law, Public Safety, Corrections & Security Cluster: youth services worker, paralegal, security systems designer, or animal control officer. Then use the following table to compare and contrast it with an occupation from another Career Cluster of your choice. Finally, tell which job would suit you best. Conduct library/Internet research to locate the necessary information.

Hint: The *Occupational Outlook Handbook* (OOH) is available in most public libraries and is a good source of career information. Your school counselor's office may also have career information available. The online version of the OOH [http://www.bls.gov/oco/] is a good starting point for Internet research.

	Law, Public Safety, Corrections & Security occupation:	**Other occupation:**
Qualifications/training		
Earnings		
Employment outlook		
Working conditions		
Typical duties		
Similar occupations		
Additional sources of information about this occupation		

Which of these two jobs would suit you better? Why?

_____

_____

ACTIVITY—EMERGENCY AND FIRE MANAGEMENT SERVICES

An **emergency medical technician (EMT)** is someone who responds to the scene of an accident or other medical emergency. EMTs give appropriate medical care and—when needed—transport the victim to the hospital. This quiz will test how familiar you are with some basic first-aid techniques all EMTs must know. (Your teacher has the correct answers to this quiz.)

1. What is the first thing you should check for with any injured person?
A bleeding
B circulation
C fractures
D blocked airway

2. A patient has a cut hand that is bleeding a lot. You should
A wrap a tourniquet around the patient's arm to stop the bleeding.
B place a sterile gauze over the wound and put pressure on it.
C put the patient's hand below her heart.
D all of the above.

3. The best method for controlling a nosebleed is to
A apply pressure to the facial artery.
B pinch the nostrils together.
C pack the nose with cotton.
D pack the nose with gauze.

4. Which of the following is a sign of shock?
A high blood pressure
B unconsciousness
C pale, cool, clammy skin
D slow pulse rate

5. You respond to a child who is having a severe allergic reaction to a bee sting. Which of the following would you use to help the child?
A an EpiPen
B acetaminophen
C insect repellent with 100% DEET
D aspirin

6. A patient has touched a hot stove and you think he has a first-degree burn. What should you do?
A Run cool water over the burned area.
B Put ice on the burn.
C Rub petroleum jelly on the burn.
D Run warm water over the burned area.

What kinds of personal characteristics does a good EMT need? How many of these characteristics do *you* have?

_____

_____

_____

Do you think you would like to be an EMT? Why or why not?

_____

_____

_____

ACTIVITY—SECURITY AND PROTECTIVE SERVICES

Shoplifting is a serious crime. It has been estimated that as many as 1 in 11 Americans have shoplifted. Retailers lose more than $13 billion worth of goods to shoplifters each year. To cover losses from theft, businesses must charge customers higher prices. Store owners must take action to control shoplifting.

In this exercise, you have been hired by a local department store to help control shoplifting. Use library and Internet resources (search keywords *shoplifting prevention*) to put together a shoplifting prevention plan for this store. Use the following questions to develop your plan.

1. Store employees can be trained to spot shoplifters. Two signs to watch for are listed below. Add three more signs that store employees should look for.

☐ Pay attention to people wearing loose-fitting, bulky clothing.

☐ Keep an eye on customers who spend more time watching the cashier or sales clerk than actually shopping.

_____

_____

_____

2. To defend against shoplifting, store employees should understand the different methods shoplifters use. Two are listed below. Add three more.

☐ Shoplifters sometimes conceal articles behind newspapers or magazines.

☐ Shoplifters sometimes wear garments out of a store.

_____

_____

_____

3. Stores should also practice good prevention techniques. Two are listed below. Add three more.

☐ Keep valuable items away from store exits to discourage "grab-and-run" thieves.

☐ Do not stack merchandise so high that sales clerks cannot see over it.

_____

_____

_____

ACTIVITY—LEGAL SERVICES

Ethics are principles and values that guide how people behave. People who act ethically try to do what is right. Attorneys must make ethical decisions every day. If you were an attorney, how would you handle the following situations?

1. You are a defense attorney. Your job is to defend people who are accused of committing crimes. Today, you take on a new client who is accused of robbing a bank. At first, he claims to be innocent, but after a few minutes of questioning he tells you, "OK, I did rob the bank. But I want to plead not guilty. My wife will swear in court that I was home at the time of the robbery." How will you respond?

_____

_____

_____

_____

2. You are a prosecuting attorney. Your job is to present evidence in court proving that the defendant (the person on trial for committing a crime) is guilty. In this case, the defendant is accused of drunk driving. You are sure that you have enough evidence to convict her of this crime. However, you know that if she is found guilty, she will lose her driver's license. This will make it hard for her to get to work every day. She has three small children who depend on her income. If you withhold some evidence, the defendant will probably receive a fine rather than losing her license. What will you do?

_____

_____

_____

_____

3. Your client was injured in an automobile accident. He tells you that he wants to sue the driver of the car that hit him. As you discuss the facts, you decide that he probably has a good chance of winning a cash settlement. But when you begin to talk about how much it will cost to hire you, he tells you that he does not have much money. Then he makes you an offer: "What if we go ahead with the lawsuit, and if we win, I'll give you half of whatever we get." How will you respond?

_____

_____

_____

_____

ACTIVITY—CORRECTION SERVICES

Over the past few decades, correction services professionals in the United States have emphasized punishment over rehabilitation (preparing prisoners to return to society after serving their sentences). Opportunities for education and job training for prisoners have received less attention. Growing crime rates have led to efforts to lengthen prison sentences and to require minimum sentences for particular crimes. With over 2 million inmates, the United States has the highest rate of incarceration in the world.

Many correction services professionals believe that prisons have become "crime factories." Inmates associate with hardened criminals all day. Aggressive behavior is routine, and even rewarded. Many people emerge from prison even more violent than when they entered. The Bureau of Justice Statistics reports that more than two-thirds of released prisoners are arrested again within three years.

Is the penal system in America "broken"? In this exercise, you will use library/Internet resources to research the topic of prison reform (keywords *prison reform*). Use your findings to answer the following questions.

1. Do you believe America's prisons have become "crime factories"? Provide evidence for your views.

_____

_____

_____

2. In the space below, tell what you believe are the two most important goals of the penal system. For example, do prisons exist mainly to punish criminals? To reform criminals? To scare people into obeying the law? Give reasons for your choices.

_____

_____

_____

3. Based on your research, describe one prison program or reform that correction services professionals are trying. For example, you might describe an educational or drug treatment program you read about.

_____

_____

_____

4. On a separate sheet of paper, write two or three paragraphs about an existing prison program that is in line with one of the goals you identified in question 2. If no such program exists, tell what you would do.

ACTIVITY—BE A DETECTIVE

Detectives solve crimes by gathering facts and information. Unfortunately, they do not always have all of the facts. Sometimes they need to figure out what happened by making inferences. An **inference** is a logical conclusion based on evidence. Detective work is often slow and methodical. Detectives must often use critical thinking and the process of elimination to arrive at the truth.

The following puzzles can be solved with the limited information given. Give them a try and find out how good your detective skills are. You get a little help for the first puzzle.

Puzzle 1

Noah, Ivy, and Bethany are friends. Each of them has a favorite color. One likes green, one likes blue, and one likes red. Your problem is to figure out who likes which color.

Colors			
Names	Green	Blue	Red
Ivy			
Noah			
Bethany			

Clues:
1. Ivy loves green. Write *YES* under green for Ivy and write *NO* under green for the others. Also write *NO* under blue and red for Ivy.
2. Bethany likes the color that begins with "B." Finish the puzzle.

Puzzle 2

Noah, Ivy, and Bethany each have a favorite flavor of ice cream. No one likes the same kind. One likes chocolate chip, one likes strawberry, and one likes vanilla. Use the clues to figure out who likes which flavor

Colors			
Names	Chocolate chip	Strawberry	Vanilla
Ivy			
Noah			
Bethany			

Clues:
1. Bethany is allergic to chocolate.
2. Noah won't eat any ice cream that has fruit.
3. Strawberry is Ivy's favorite flavor.

ACTIVITY— EMERGENCY AND FIRE MANAGEMENT SERVICES

http://www.wildlandfire.com

Wildland firefighters help control and suppress forest fires and other blazes that occur in natural areas. Visit the wildlandfire.com Web site or use other library/Internet resources (keyword *wildland firefighter*) to learn more about this demanding profession. Then answer the following questions.

1. Find a news story about a recent wildfire. Where did it occur? How far is that from your community?

_____

_____

_____

2. What is a red card and how do you get one?

_____

_____

_____

3. What kind of equipment do wildland firefighters typically use on the job?

_____

_____

_____

4. What is the "pack test"? What do you need to do to pass the pack test?

_____

_____

_____

5. Do you think you would enjoy working as a wildland firefighter? Why or why not?

_____

_____

_____

ACTIVITY—OUR LIVING CONSTITUTION

The U.S. Constitution is the basis for the laws in our society. Therefore, all Americans need to understand how the constitution applies to our everyday lives.

1. The following situations are real-world applications of some of the 26 amendments to the constitution. Use library or Internet research to determine which amendment governs the situation given and put the number of the amendment in the blank.

_____ George W. Bush was elected president twice. Which amendment prevents him from being elected to a third term?

_____ Americans cannot be forced to let soldiers live in their homes if they do not want them there. This right is a part of which constitutional amendment?

_____ Mark Conner is arrested for stealing his elderly neighbor's purse, which contained $5.50. At the police station, the arresting officer tells Mark that he's going to jail for life for his crime. Mark knows that he has done wrong, but he is also certain that he cannot receive a life sentence for stealing such a small amount. Which amendment makes Mark so sure?

_____ Bob Plum is a police officer. He goes to Otis Jackson's house and demands to be let inside. Officer Plum has no reason to think that Jackson has done anything wrong; he just wants to "look around" to be sure. Jackson shouts to the officer, "Go away! You don't have a search warrant!" Which constitutional amendment gives Jackson this protection?

_____ Donna Collingwood tells the police that she saw John Marr rob the First National Bank. Later, Collingwood refuses to testify to this statement in court, so her statement cannot be admitted as evidence against Marr. This is because a defendant has the right to be confronted by those who accuse him. Where in the constitution is this stated?

_____ Eighteen-year-old Midori Lee is about to vote in her first presidential election. Which amendment gives her this right?

_____ One evening, Spreen's car collides with Manning's car. Spreen says Manning's car ran a red light. Manning, who is a deputy sheriff, says Spreen's car ran the red light. Spreen was not hurt, but he decides to sue Manning for damages for his car. Spreen is afraid that the judge will believe Manning because he is a sheriff. However, he has faith that 12 impartial observers will decide in his favor; therefore, he demands a jury trial. Where in the constitution is Spreen guaranteed this right?

2. Now that you have read through the amendments to the constitution, use a separate sheet of paper to rank the ten you believe are the most important. Provide an explanation for each selection.

EXPLORING A CAREER IN THE LAW, PUBLIC SAFETY, CORRECTIONS & SECURITY CLUSTER

The O*NET program (http://online.onetcenter.org/) is the nation's primary source of occupational information. O*NET provides data on thousands of specific jobs, including typical tasks, knowledge/skills, work styles, and education required by each. Visit the O*NET site to complete this activity. (If you do not have Internet access, gather information from your library's print version of the *Occupational Outlook Handbook*.)

1. Click the Find Occupations link. In the Quick Search box, enter a job title from the Law, Public Safety, Corrections & Security Career Cluster that interests you. View the Details report.

(*Note:* Sample occupations in this Career Cluster can be found at the www.careerclusters.org Web site or from your teacher.)

2. Use the information you find at O*NET to fill out the following chart for the job title you chose. List the top three characteristics of the items with an asterisk (*).

Tasks*	Tools & Technology*	Knowledge*	Skills*
Abilities*	Work Activities*	Work Context*	Interests*
Work Styles*	Work Values*	Work Needs*	Related Occupations
Education Required	Median Wages	Employment	Projected Growth

3. Would you be interested in this job? Why or why not?

_____

_____

_____

Passions
☐ Working with people
☐ Solving problems
☐ Helping others

Attitude
☐ People-oriented
☐ Caring

Talents
☐ Ability to speak in public
☐ Communication skills
☐ Ability to lead and facilitate

Heart
☐ Likes to improve how things work
☐ Likes to communicate with all types of people

Some Career Areas to Consider
☐ Postal worker
☐ City planner
☐ Legislative assistant
☐ Foreign service officer
☐ Building inspector

Employment Outlook
☐ Jobs in state and local government are expected to increase about 10 percent in the next ten years.
☐ Competition for jobs in foreign service is high.
☐ Job growth in revenue and taxation is expected to be slow, while faster growth is expected in the regulatory industry.

ACTIVITY—FOREIGN SERVICE

Laura comes from Chicago. She is currently living and working in Abidjan, Côte d'Ivoire, in Africa. She says, "I love that I am able to learn languages and live in other countries. I also enjoy the interactions I have daily with the public. I have the opportunity to meet different people from educators and government officials to farmers and lawyers." Do you and Laura share similar interests? If so, a career in the foreign service may be right for you.

As a foreign service officer, you could be assigned to an embassy or consulate anywhere in the world. Your post may be a large city in Egypt or in a remote area of Kenya. Some posts can be dangerous, such as in areas experiencing civil war. Living conditions and medical facilities in some regions fall far short of American standards. The area may lack electricity and easy access to fresh water. As a result, all American foreign service officers must be prepared for a variety of living conditions and meet strict standards for medical fitness. In areas that are politically unstable, your family may not be able to accompany you.

The foreign service offers five career tracks. Here are some examples of duties performed by employees in each track:

Consular officers help U.S. citizens traveling abroad with problems such as lost passports and medical emergencies. They also interview foreign citizens who want to travel to the United States and decide whether to grant the foreigners a visa to enter.

☐ **Economic officers** negotiate trade agreements with foreign countries and resolve trade disputes. Some help foreign countries develop a free-market economy.

☐ **Management officers** train and supervise workers at U.S. embassies and consulates. To rise to this position, they must have several years of experience working in a consulate.

☐ **Political officers** analyze political events in a region and make recommendations on foreign policy. They engage in negotiations and advise decision-makers.

☐ **Public diplomacy officers** use media outlets to educate foreign citizens about American society. They explain American history and values to foreign audiences. They conduct exchange programs to promote mutual understanding.

Directions: Use the information from the article and your own experiences to answer the following questions.

1. **Evaluating** What aspects of a foreign service job would excite you?

_____

_____

_____

_____

_____

2. **Identifying** What are some of the challenges of working as a foreign service officer?

_____

_____

_____

_____

3. **Differentiating** Which of the five career tracks is particularly concerned with promoting a positive image of the United States? How?

_____

_____

_____

_____

4. **Making Connections** In what area of the world would you most like to work? Why?

_____

_____

_____

_____

_____

5. **Evaluating** Do you think a career in foreign service might be right for you? Fill out the questionnaire at this Web site sponsored by the U.S. Department of State: http://careers.state.gov/resources/foreign-service-right.html. What are your results?

_____

_____

_____

_____

_____

6. **Assessing** Based on the article and the questionnaire, what kinds of personal characteristics does a foreign service employee need? Which of these characteristics do _you_ have?

_____

_____

_____

_____

_____

ORGANIZING CAREER CHOICES

Directions: Choose one of the following occupations from the Government & Public Administration Cluster: fire inspector, city council member, infantry officer, or tax examiner. Then use the following table to compare and contrast it with an occupation from another Career Cluster of your choice. Finally, tell which job would suit you best. Conduct library/Internet research to locate the necessary information.

Hint: The *Occupational Outlook Handbook* (OOH) is available in most public libraries and is a good source of career information. Your school counselor's office may also have career information available. The online version of the OOH [http://www.bls.gov/oco/] is a good starting point for Internet research.

	Government & Public Administration occupation:	**Other occupation:**
Qualifications/training		
Earnings		
Employment outlook		
Working conditions		
Typical duties		
Similar occupations		
Additional sources of information about this occupation		

Which of these two jobs would suit you better? Why?

_____

_____

ACTIVITY—PUBLIC MANAGEMENT AND ADMINISTRATION

You are a member of your city council. New businesses in your community have brought in more tax revenue. Now the city council must decide how to use the money to benefit the community. Council has narrowed the options to two proposals: install lights on four residential streets or add a skateboard arena to the local park. You want to analyze these proposals to decide which to support.

1. How would the community benefit from the street lights?

_____

_____

_____

2. Who might oppose the lights? Why?

_____

_____

_____

3. How would the community benefit from the skateboard arena?

_____

_____

_____

4. Who might oppose the arena? Why?

_____

_____

_____

_____

5. Which proposal would you support? Why?

_____

_____

_____

ACTIVITY—REGULATION

http://www.eia.doe.gov

A **regulation** is a rule or law. Governments make regulations to control conduct in certain industries to ensure honesty or to protect public health and the environment. For example, some of our electricity comes from nuclear energy. Nuclear energy has many advantages. However, it also poses serious threats. Nuclear regulators inspect nuclear power plants to make sure they conform to government regulations. Visit the Energy Information Administration Web site—and do additional library/Internet research about nuclear energy—to answer the following questions. (Hint: From the EIA home page, click the Energy Kid's Page link, then Energy Facts.)

1. What is nuclear energy?

_____

_____

_____

2. What are some advantages of using nuclear energy to produce electricity?

_____

_____

_____

_____

3. How does nuclear energy pose a threat to the environment and public health?

_____

_____

_____

_____

4. What rules must power plants follow for safely disposing of nuclear waste?

_____

_____

_____

_____

ACTIVITY—GOVERNANCE

http://clerkkids.house.gov/

Do you know how laws are made in the U.S. Congress? Go to the "Kids in the House" Web site (click the How Laws Are Made link) or do library research to learn about the steps in the lawmaking process. Then take this quiz. (Your teacher has the correct answers.)

1. Who can sponsor legislation?
A anyone
B only a member of Congress
C only the President of the United States
D only a Supreme Court justice

2. When legislation is first introduced in Congress, what is it called?
A an act
B a bill
C an enrolled bill
D a constituent

3. What happens to proposed legislation that has been tabled?
A It dies.
B It is referred to a standing committee.
C It is referred to a subcommittee.
D It goes to the President to be signed.

4. What does a conference committee do with proposed legislation?
A study it carefully and hold hearings with experts
B add amendments to it
C vote on whether to override the President's veto of it
D resolve differences between House and Senate versions

5. How many votes are required to override the President's veto?
A two thirds of the members of the House of Representatives
B two thirds of the members of both houses
C half of the members of the Senate
D half of the members of both houses

6. When does proposed legislation become a law?
A when it passes either the Senate or the House of Representatives
B when it passes both the Senate and the House of Representatives
C when it passes both houses and the President signs it
D when the President uses the pocket veto

ACTIVITY—PLANNING

http://factfinder.census.gov/

Every ten years the U.S. Census Bureau sends a survey form to all American households. The survey collects information about you and your family, such as how many people live in your house, how many males and females, and how old they are. Census takers visit households that have not returned the survey form to interview the residents and complete the form. After the information is collected, it is compiled into tables and graphs. Governments use the information to plan for community needs. For example, if your city has more young children now than it did ten years ago, the city manager might make plans to build a new school.

Go to the Census Bureau Fun Facts Web site and click on your state, or find census data for 1990 and 2000 for your state in the library. (Hint: From the home page, click the Kid's Corner link, then click Facts.) Then answer the following questions.

1. Did the total population of your state increase or decrease between 1990 and 2000? By how much?

_____

_____

2. In 2000, did most people in your state live in cities (urban) or in the country (rural)?

_____

_____

3. "Median age" means that half the people are older and half are younger. It is a type of average. Did the median age in your state increase or decrease between 1990 and 2000? What does this trend say about the population of your state?

_____

_____

_____

4. Suppose a company that makes diapers and baby food wants to expand its advertising to a new market area. Would your state be a good place for this company to target its advertising? Why or why not?

_____

_____

_____

_____

ACTIVITY—NATIONAL SECURITY

In 1972, a plane took off from JFK Airport in New York. Moments later, the airport received a warning that a bomb was aboard. The plane returned to the airport and the passengers were evacuated. Then Brandy, a bomb-sniffing dog, was sent in. Brandy found the bomb just 12 minutes before it was set to explode. That same day, the President directed the Federal Aviation Administration to start a program to train more teams of dogs and handlers to work at airports.

Today, the Transportation Security Administration (TSA) runs a training program for canine teams. After graduation, the teams patrol airports as employees of the city, county, state, or airport law enforcement authority. They are not employees of TSA. To learn how the dogs are trained, do library research or go to the TSA Web site http://www.tsa.gov/what_we_do/ and click the link to "Canine Explosive Detection Teams." Then answer these questions.

1. Why are dogs used to detect bombs?

_____

_____

_____

2. What are dogs trained to detect? What do they receive when they succeed?

_____

_____

_____

3. What are dogs trained to do when they find an explosive device? Why is it important for the dog to respond "passively"?

_____

_____

_____

4. Do you think you would like to work as part of a canine bomb-detection team? Why or why not?

_____

_____

_____

_____

ACTIVITY—REVENUE AND TAXATION

If you wanted to buy national defense, could you? National defense—or, more specifically, the military that provides it—is one of the many public goods funded by the government. **Public goods** are goods and services available to everyone in a society. Public goods include police, roads, street lights, parks, and schools. Everyone can benefit from these public goods because each of us pays part of the cost through our taxes.

All levels of government provide public goods. The federal government funds programs that benefit the country as a whole, such as interstate highways and national parks. State and local governments pay for services to local communities, such as schools, firefighters, local parks, and neighborhood streets.

Employees of the Internal Revenue Service (IRS) are responsible for collecting and processing taxes. Tax laws are complex and they change a bit each year. Tax examiners learn the tax laws so they can answer questions from taxpayers and review tax returns for accuracy. The IRS also employs special agents to investigate unlawful schemes to evade taxes. Do online or library research to learn more about taxes and related jobs. Then answer these questions.

1. How would your community be different if no one paid taxes?

_____

_____

_____

2. Name three public goods in your community that you have used in the last month.

_____

_____

3. If you made a mistake on your tax return, would the IRS prosecute you for a crime? Why or why not? (*Hint:* Look up "tax avoidance" and "tax evasion" to determine the difference.)

_____

_____

_____

4. What personal characteristics would a good tax examiner need? What additional characteristics would an IRS criminal investigator need? Do you think you would like either of these jobs? Why or why not?

_____

_____

_____

ACTIVITY—CONGRESSIONAL PAGES

Do you think you would like to be a politician? Would you like a first-hand glimpse of what members of Congress do? Then you might want to seek a job as a congressional page.

Each year Congress hires approximately 100 high school juniors from across the nation to serve as pages. Students must be at least 16 and must be sponsored by their local representative or senator. Competition is intense. Grade point average is a major consideration in the selection process. To be considered, students must make a request to their representative or senator.

Part of the reason for the page program is to groom interested students for a career in government service. In fact, several current and former members of Congress were once pages.

For pages, the day begins at 6:45 a.m., when they attend classes at Page School. The workday begins just after classes end, around 9:00 a.m., and continues until 5:00 p.m. Pages serve mostly as messengers. They carry documents between congressional offices. They prepare House and Senate chambers for the day's work by distributing the *Congressional Record* and other documents related to the agenda. When Congress is meeting, pages sit near their representatives, who will summon them for assistance as needed.

Pages wear a uniform, which includes a navy blazer and tie for both males and females. All pages live together in triple rooms at the Page Residence Hall, under the supervision of a resident manager and proctors. Pages must agree in writing to a strict code of conduct, which includes a curfew. Pages receive a small salary, but the most valuable pay is the experience they gain from witnessing—and participating in—our government in action.

1. How do you think a job as a congressional page could help prepare you for a career in government?

_____

_____

2. What personal characteristics do you have that would make you a good page?

_____

_____

3. Do library or online research to identify the name of your representative in the House of Representatives. On a separate sheet of paper, compose a letter to your representative, describing why you want to be a page and your qualifications for the job. Remember—You will have plenty of competition. Try to convey your excitement. Also, give details about yourself that will help your qualifications stand out.

EXPLORING A CAREER IN THE GOVERNMENT & PUBLIC ADMINISTRATION CLUSTER

The O*NET program (http://online.onetcenter.org/) is the nation's primary source of occupational information. O*NET provides data on thousands of specific jobs, including typical tasks, knowledge/skills, work styles, and education required by each. Visit the O*NET site to complete this activity. (If you do not have Internet access, gather information from your library's print version of the *Occupational Outlook Handbook*.)

1. Click the Find Occupations link. In the Quick Search box, enter a job title from the Government & Public Administration Career Cluster that interests you. View the Details report.

(*Note:* Sample occupations in this Career Cluster can be found at the www.careerclusters.org Web site or from your teacher.)

2. Use the information you find at O*NET to fill out the following chart for the job title you chose. List the top three characteristics of the items with an asterisk (*).

Tasks*	Tools & Technology*	Knowledge*	Skills*
Abilities*	Work Activities*	Work Context*	Interests*
Work Styles*	Work Values*	Work Needs*	Related Occupations
Education Required	Median Wages	Employment	Projected Growth

3. Would you be interested in this job? Why or why not?

_____

_____

Passions
- ☐ Working with people
- ☐ Fascinated with human nature
- ☐ Helping others

Attitude
- ☐ Dependable
- ☐ Respected by others

Talents
- ☐ Communication skills
- ☐ Ability to work with all types of people
- ☐ Understanding of human nature

Heart
- ☐ Wants to understand others' situations
- ☐ Wants to make things better for others

Some Career Areas to Consider
- ☐ Funeral director
- ☐ Social worker
- ☐ Psychologist
- ☐ Nanny
- ☐ Career counselor

Employment Outlook
- ☐ More than 7 million people are employed in human services occupations. Faster-than-average employment growth is expected in this Cluster.
- ☐ High turnover should create numerous employment opportunities in human services, particularly in childcare positions. Many fast-growing occupations exist in social services, especially those that involve working with the elderly.

ACTIVITY—COUNSELING AND MENTAL HEALTH SERVICES

Defense mechanisms are unconscious psychological strategies people use when they are under stress to cope with a situation and to reduce the unpleasant feelings associated with it. Psychologists have identified several defense mechanisms. Some of the most common are listed below:

- ☐ *Denial*: stating that an unpleasant situation simply does not exist. (Example: An actor who was caught using marijuana says she doesn't have a drug problem.)
- ☐ *Displacement*: shifting negative or aggressive feelings from a dangerous target to a safe one. (Example: You yell at the dog after having a fight with your mom.)
- ☐ *Humor*: making a joke out of an unpleasant thought or experience. (Example: You tell a long, funny story about a time you crashed on your skateboard and broke your arm.)
- ☐ *Intellectualization*: overthinking a problem or focusing on facts and logic to get distance from an unpleasant feeling or event. (Example: When your grandmother dies, you focus on the details of her funeral rather than on your own sadness.)

- *Projection*: transferring your own unacceptable feelings onto someone else. (Example: You are angry with your sister, but you insist that your mom is the one who is angry.)
- *Reaction formation*: transforming negative, dangerous, or unpleasant feelings or beliefs into their opposites. (Example: You strongly dislike your aunt, but every time she visits you rush to give her a big hug.)
- *Repression*: pulling a bad memory into the unconscious. (Example: You completely forget about the time a friend spread gossip about you.)
- *Sublimation*: converting negative feelings into positive actions. (Example: You jog for 10 extra minutes to blow off steam after getting an F on a test.)

Everyone uses defense mechanisms, but some are considered more emotionally healthy and mature than others. For example, *anticipation* involves planning to cope with a future stressful event. It is not pleasant to think about growing old or dying, but responsible adults make plans—such as purchasing life insurance or having a will made—so they will be prepared when the time comes.

When psychologists counsel clients, they must understand the various defense mechanisms their clients may be using. This knowledge can help a psychologist move a client past the defense mechanism and confront what is really wrong. allowing the client to become a stronger, healthier individual.

Directions: Use the information from the article and your own experiences to answer the following questions.

1. **Defining** What is a defense mechanism?

_____

_____

_____

_____

2. **Explaining** How can knowing about the different kinds of defense mechanisms help psychologists treat their clients?

_____

_____

_____

_____

_____

3. **Identifying** Suppose Ben's doctor has diagnosed him with cancer. Ben tells the doctor that she is wrong and demands a second opinion. Which defense mechanism is Ben using in this situation?

_____

_____

_____

_____

4. **Classifying** Of the defense mechanisms listed in the article, which do you think are most likely to be used by a mature, psychologically healthy person? Explain your answer.

_____

_____

_____

_____

5. **Analyzing** Describe a time you or someone you know used one of the defense mechanisms listed in the article. What happened? Did the defense mechanism make the situation better or worse?

_____

_____

_____

_____

6. **Assessing** Based on the article, what kinds of personal characteristics does a good psychologist need? How many of these characteristics do *you* have?

_____

_____

_____

_____

ORGANIZING CAREER CHOICES

Directions: Choose one of the following occupations from the Human Services Cluster: preschool teacher, marriage counselor, adult day care worker, personal trainer, or certified financial planner. Then use the following table to compare and contrast it with an occupation from another Career Cluster of your choice. Finally, tell which job would suit you best. Conduct library/Internet research to locate the necessary information.

Hint: The *Occupational Outlook Handbook* (OOH) is available in most public libraries and is a good source of career information. Your school counselor's office may also have career information available. The online version of the OOH [http://www.bls.gov/oco/] is a good starting point for Internet research.

	Human Services occupation:	**Other occupation:**
Qualifications/training		
Earnings		
Employment outlook		
Working conditions		
Typical duties		
Similar occupations		
Additional sources of information about this occupation		

Which of these two jobs would suit you better? Why?

_____

_____

ACTIVITY—PERSONAL CARE SERVICES

Do you like to keep up on the latest hairstyle trends? Do you know the difference between a brush cut and a fade? Then maybe a career in cosmetology is for you. A **cosmetologist** cuts and styles hair, performs manicures, and offers makeup advice. In this activity, you are going to suggest a different hairstyle for a friend or family member.

1. First, you need to learn a bit about how to match hairstyle with facial shape. The table below lists several common facial shapes. Do some library/Internet research (keyword *facial shapes hairstyle*) to find out which types of hairstyles go well with each.

Facial shape	Good hairstyle choices
Oval	
Square	
Round	
Diamond	
Pear	
Heart	
Rectangle	

2. In the space below, identify the person for whom you are going to suggest a new hairstyle and tell his or her facial shape.

_____

_____

3. Now you need to get some hairstyle ideas. Go online to look for some examples (use the keyword *hairstyles*) or look through some fashion magazines at the library. When you find the right hairstyle for your friend, print out or make a copy of the picture. Then explain why you think this style is right for your friend.

_____

_____

4. Finally, show the picture to your friend. Did he/she like your choice? Why or why not?

_____

ACTIVITY—FAMILY AND COMMUNITY SERVICES

In this activity, you are a community services worker helping the Montez family (father, mother, 18-month old girl, 7-year-old boy), whose house and possessions have been destroyed by a fire. The Montezes lost everything but the clothes they were wearing when they escaped the burning house. The family is living with relatives while they try to get back on their feet.

Your organization has already established a fund at a local bank to accept cash donations from people who want to help the Montez family. Today you will (a) generate a list of basic items the family needs and (b) approach a local business to donate an item or service from that list.

1. Use the table below to create a list of things this family needs right away. Focus only on items or services the Montezes *must* have—not on "extras" such as DVDs or a video game system. Use newspaper ads or other similar resources to estimate the cost of each item you identify.

Basic Family Need	Estimated Cost	Basic Family Need	Estimated Cost

2. Now find a local business that sells a product or service the Montezes need. On a separate sheet of paper, write a letter to this business asking for a donation. You may want to examine some fundraising letter samples online or in the library (keywords *fundraising letter*) before you write your letter, to get some tips on how best to approach a business for a donation.

ACTIVITY—COUNSELING AND MENTAL HEALTH SERVICES

A **counselor** is someone who gives advice. Counselors often need to help their clients find ways to identify the consequences of everyday conflicts and find ways to deal with them. In this activity, you and a partner are going to take turns being the counselor and the client as you discuss a personal conflict or problem.

You and your partner will need to decide who will be the counselor first and who will be the client. (You will switch roles later.) The counselor should ask the client the following questions and record the answers in the spaces provided.

1. Tell me about a frustrating situation you have experienced. Describe the situation.

_____

_____

_____

2. How did you handle the situation? What happened because of the way you dealt with it?

_____

_____

_____

3. If you could go back and change your behavior, would you? How?

_____

_____

_____

Now, generate some ideas in the space below to share with your client about other ways he or she might have handled the situation (for example, listening more closely, apologizing, compromising, getting help from another person). Talk about your ideas with your client and ask him or her to come up with some as well.

_____

_____

_____

_____

4. After you have finished your work as counselor, switch roles and repeat the procedure.

ACTIVITY—EARLY CHILDHOOD DEVELOPMENT AND SERVICES

A **nanny** is someone hired by a family to take care of the children. Nannies can work full or part time and generally care for children from infancy to about age 12. They often live with the families that hire them, tending to the children's early education, nutrition, health, and other needs. Nannies may also perform housekeeping duties related to the children, such as cleaning their rooms or doing their laundry. A nanny is not responsible for caring for adult family members.

In this activity, you will read several situations a nanny might face. Before answering the questions, do some library or online research about a nanny's duties. Then, in the space provided, tell how you would handle each situation.

1. Jacob is seven years old. His parents have him on a strict no-sugar diet. Today, as you return from the grocery store, Jacob runs to you and begins searching through the bags to see what you have brought home. You have bought yourself a package of cookies you hoped to enjoy in your room later. Jacob sees the cookies, and of course wants them for himself. What will you do?

_____

_____

_____

_____

_____

2. You are a live-in nanny for the Mortimer family. On your day off, you receive a phone call from Mrs. Mortimer, who explains that she is caught in traffic and will not get home in time to cook Mr. Mortimer's dinner. She instructs you to make dinner for him. What will you do?

_____

_____

_____

_____

3. Ten-year-old Ryan's room is a mess. You ask her to clean her room and she laughs at you, saying, "That's your job. You're the nanny. _You_ do it." What will you do?

_____

_____

_____

_____

ACTIVITY—CONSUMER SERVICES

A **lemon** is a nickname for a vehicle that is found to be defective or unsatisfactory after it is purchased. A lemon's defects are usually not apparent until after the customer buys the vehicle. **Lemon laws** are state consumer laws that offer remedies to customers who have bought defective vehicles. There is also a federal lemon law—the Magnuson-Moss Warranty Act. Lemon laws vary by state.

In this exercise, you are going to take on the role of a consumer advocate advising someone who has purchased a lemon.

1. First, use the space below to explain the purpose of lemon laws to your client.

_____

_____

_____

_____

2. Now do some online or library research about your state's lemon law (keywords *[your state's name] lemon law*). In the space below, explain the scope of the law's protection and when, why, and how your client can use it.

_____

_____

_____

_____

_____

_____

3. Suppose a second client wants to hire you to help file a lemon law complaint. She tells you that she purchased a used car "as is" from a local auto dealership. Can she file a lemon law complaint? Explain.

_____

_____

_____

_____

_____

ACTIVITY—PERSONAL CARE SERVCIES

A **personal trainer** educates people about physical fitness. Personal trainers evaluate their clients' fitness levels and help them work out a fitness program to help them safely achieve their personal goals. They also provide information about diet and good nutrition.

Do you think you have what it takes to become a personal trainer? Take this quiz to find out. (Your teacher has the answers to this test.)

1. The safest way to lose weight is to
A go on a diet.
B do a lot of sit-ups.
C sit in a hot sauna every day.
D exercise and eat a healthy diet.

2. Which of the following is an example of an anaerobic activity?
A bicycling
B lifting weights
C swimming
D jogging

3. If you want to achieve a "six-pack," you should
A do 300 deep-knee bends every day.
B do 500 crunches every day.
C reduce your overall body fat.
D drink lots of water.

4. You decide to increase your level of cardiorespiratory endurance. Which exercise will help you achieve your goal?
A dumbbell curls
B jumping rope
C pushups
D sit-ups

5. Strengthening your abdominal muscles is one of the best ways to
A lose fat in your abdominal region.
B improve your skin quality.
C protect against back pain.
D ensure better breathing.

6. When lifting weights, you should _____ when your muscles contract and _____ when they lengthen.
A inhale/exhale
B exhale/inhale
C hold my breath/exhale
D inhale/hold my breath

7. Use library or Internet resources to find three exercises a personal trainer could recommend to a healthy, 30-year-old client who wanted to develop her upper body strength.

_____

_____

_____

8. Based on how well you did on this quiz, do you think you would make a good personal trainer? Why or why not?

_____

_____

ACTIVITY—CONSUMER SERVICES

Financial planners analyze their clients' overall financial situations and develop plans to meet their goals and objectives. Today you are helping Angela Rice evaluate three popular retirement plans: a Traditional IRA, a Roth IRA, and a 401(k) plan. Planning for retirement can be difficult and confusing, so Angela wants an easy-to-understand document that will help her quickly identify differences and similarities among the three plans.

1. Use library or Internet research to complete the table about the key features of each retirement plan. You will present this information to your client.

	Traditional IRA	**Roth IRA**	**401(k)**
Does the individual or employer set up?			
Income limits			
Contribution limits			
Matching contributions			
Distributions			
Forced distributions			
Tax implications			
Early withdrawal penalties			
Other key features			

2. What kinds of personal characteristics does a good financial planner need? How many of these characteristics do *you* have?

_____

_____

_____

EXPLORING A CAREER IN THE HUMAN SERVICES CLUSTER

The O*NET program (http://online.onetcenter.org/) is the nation's primary source of occupational information. O*NET provides data on thousands of specific jobs, including typical tasks, knowledge/skills, work styles, and education required by each. Visit the O*NET site to complete this activity. (If you do not have Internet access, gather information from your library's print version of the *Occupational Outlook Handbook*.)

1. Click the Find Occupations link. In the Quick Search box, enter a job title from the Human Services Career Cluster that interests you. View the Details report.

(*Note:* Sample occupations in this Career Cluster can be found at the www.careerclusters.org Web site or from your teacher.)

2. Use the information you find at O*NET to fill out the following chart for the job title you chose. List the top three characteristics of the items with an asterisk (*).

Tasks*	Tools & Technology*	Knowledge*	Skills*
Abilities*	Work Activities*	Work Context*	Interests*
Work Styles*	Work Values*	Work Needs*	Related Occupations
Education Required	Median Wages	Employment	Projected Growth

3. Would you be interested in this job? Why or why not?

_____

_____

_____

Passions

☐ Interacting with others

☐ Leading or teaching

☐ Understanding others' needs

Attitude

☐ Caring

☐ Outgoing

Talents

☐ Ability to work with all types of people

☐ Planning and organizing ability

☐ Good verbal skills

Heart

☐ Likes to help people

☐ Likes to work closely with others

Some Career Areas to Consider

☐ Childcare worker

☐ Instructional media designer

☐ Teacher

☐ College professor

☐ Speech-language pathologist

Employment Outlook

☐ Job opportunities for teachers and administrators are expected to be excellent over the next 10 years.

☐ Jobs in professional support services are expected to experience better than average growth through 2012.

ACTIVITY—TEACHING AND TRAINING

If you attended a traditional elementary school, you probably learned by listening to the teacher, doing required activities, and taking tests. In the late 1800s and early 1900s, Maria Montessori, an Italian educator, developed a different way to help children learn. Through her research, Montessori observed that children are naturally creative and curious. She concluded that children learn best from directing their own learning activities. Montessori developed materials for a learning environment and a teaching method to enable self-directed learning.

A Montessori classroom is well stocked with learning materials arranged by subject area, such as math, language, science, and music. Children do not sit at desks. They are free to move around the room to work with any materials they choose. There are no textbooks. Children learn through exploration and discovery rather than from the teacher. Classes include children in three-year age groups (3-6, 6-9, 9-12). As the children interact, older children share their knowledge with younger children.

Children learn at their own pace. Seldom will two or more children be learning the same thing at the same time. The Montessori teacher works with one child at a time. Lessons are seldom given to the whole class. The children do not take tests or turn in papers for the teacher to grade.

The role of the teacher is to observe each child's progress and provide new materials when the individual child demonstrates mastery of a skill and is ready to move on.

The Montessori method emphasizes learning through the five senses. For example, students learn the alphabet using sandpaper letters. The teacher cuts letters of the alphabet out of fine sandpaper and mounts them, well spaced, on a stiff card. The card containing vowels is colored differently from the card containing consonants. Instead of memorizing the names of letters at first, students learn their sounds. For example, the teacher would introduce the letter "T" as "tuh." Using this method, children learn each letter through three senses: hearing the sound, seeing the form, and feeling its shape by tracing its rough surface with their fingers. The muscle memory created by tracing helps children move on to handwriting when they are ready.

To become a Montessori teacher, you must earn certification from a Montessori training school. During training, you will learn how to prepare the classroom according to Montessori principles and use lesson materials. You will also learn how to recognize when a child is ready to advance and how to guide individual progress.

> "It is so difficult to keep from over-directing, to observe without judgment, to wait for the child to reveal herself. Yet, over and over again, when we do honor that inner guide, the personality unfolds in a way that surprises—that goes beyond what we could direct or predict."
>
> —Professor Sharon Dubble, Ph.D., Loyola College in Maryland

Directions: Use the information from the article and your own experiences to answer the following questions.

1. **Identifying** Who was Maria Montessori?

_____

_____

_____

_____

_____

2. **Describing** What is a Montessori classroom like?

_____

_____

_____

_____

_____

3. **Explaining** How do children learn in a Montessori classroom?

_____

_____

_____

_____

_____

4. **Analyzing** After a child has learned the alphabet using sandpaper letters, how would you change the materials to help the child learn how to create words?

_____

_____

_____

_____

_____

5. **Contrasting** How is the role of a Montessori teacher different from that of a teacher in a traditional school?

_____

_____

_____

_____

_____

6. **Assessing** Based on the article, what kinds of personal characteristics does a good Montessori teacher need? Which of these characteristics do *you* have?

_____

_____

_____

_____

_____

ORGANIZING CAREER CHOICES

Directions: Choose one of the following occupations from the Education & Training Cluster: special education teacher, school psychologist, audiologist, or teacher aide. Then use the following table to compare and contrast it with an occupation from another Career Cluster of your choice. Finally, tell which job would suit you best. Conduct library/Internet research to locate the necessary information.

Hint: The *Occupational Outlook Handbook* (OOH) is available in most public libraries and is a good source of career information. Your school counselor's office may also have career information available. The online version of the OOH [http://www.bls.gov/oco/] is a good starting point for Internet research.

	Education & Training occupation:	**Other occupation:**
Qualifications/training		
Earnings		
Employment outlook		
Working conditions		
Typical duties		
Similar occupations		
Additional sources of information about this occupation		

Which of these two jobs would suit you better? Why?

_____

_____

ACTIVITY—PROFESSIONAL SUPPORT SERVICES

You are the guidance counselor at Central Middle School. An important part of your job is to help students with social and behavioral problems. You are worried about Elena. She is a new student. When she arrived at the beginning of the school year, she seemed to be adjusting well. She earned good grades and participated in school activities. Lately, however, her behavior has changed. Her grades have dipped sharply and she has become withdrawn. You seldom see her socializing with other students.

You call Elena to your office. At first she sits quietly, refusing to answer questions with more than a word or two. Soon Elena begins to cry. "Jeremy calls me names and spreads rumors about me," she says. "Jeremy says I will never be popular at this school because I am Latina. He tells everyone not to talk to me." You recognize the problem. Elena is a victim of bullying.

1. What advice would you give Elena? Explain why.

_____

_____

_____

_____

2. Do you think students should accept bullying as just a natural part of growing up? Why or why not?

_____

_____

_____

_____

3. What kinds of bullying have you observed or have happened to you?

_____

_____

_____

_____

4. What actions did you or the bullied person take in these situations? Did these actions help?

_____

_____

_____

_____

ACTIVITY—ADMINISTRATION AND ADMINISTRATIVE SUPPORT

You are the director of admissions for Homestate College. Your job is to recruit students for your college. You evaluate the qualifications of high school students who apply and decide who to admit. You work closely with the director of financial aid to help qualified students obtain scholarships and loans that will help them attend your college.

Today you are preparing for a recruiting fair for high school students to be held at a convention center. You will have a booth with brochures to hand out. You want to create a poster that will attract students to your booth. Other colleges will have booths there as well, so you want your display to stand out from the crowd.

Look at college brochures or college Web sites to see how colleges try to attract potential students. Then answer the questions below.

1. List three characteristics of a college that students in your school would find most attractive.

_____

_____

_____

2. What kinds of illustrations would you include on a recruiting poster?

_____

_____

3. Create a one-page recruiting poster for Homestate College. You can use word processing, presentation, or desktop publishing software; or sketch the poster on a piece of paper. Focus on the three important characteristics you identified in question 1. Write text for the poster based on these characteristics. Include images that illustrate the characteristics. You can download images from the Internet or cut them out of college brochures or other print publications. Fasten your poster to a stiff backing and display it in your classroom.

4. Based on this activity, do you think you would like to work in a college admissions office? Why or why not?

_____

_____

_____

_____

ACTIVITY—EARLY CHILDHOOD DEVELOPMENT

http://www.pbs.org/wholechild/abc/

Researchers in early childhood development have identified milestones that children pass through as they develop. Some milestones are physical. For example, at three to six months of age, a baby usually becomes capable of rolling over. Other milestones involve thinking skills, social skills, or communication skills. Children develop at different rates, so they do not reach each milestone at exactly the same time. However, the age ranges help parents, teachers, and childcare workers plan activities that are appropriate for a child's developmental stage. These milestones also help adult caregivers recognize possible problems, such as autism or speech difficulties, so they can seek help for the child.

You are a childcare worker. The children at your daycare center range from three months to five years of age. Visit the Web site above and read about milestones in physical development, social development, thinking skills, and communication skills. Then answer the following questions.

1. Jamal is three years old, but he cannot count to five. Should you alert his parents that he may have a learning disability? Why or why not?

_____

_____

_____

2. Dana is crawling around and grabbing whatever she can reach. What type of development is Dana displaying? About what age is Dana?

_____

_____

_____

3. Carmen is two years old. You would like Carmen to learn how to share her toys with other children. Is this a reasonable expectation for Carmen? Why or why not?

_____

_____

_____

4. Plan an activity for the children at your center who are between three and four years old. The activity should be appropriate for their developmental level. Describe the activity on a separate page.

ACTIVITY—TEACHING AND TRAINING

Teachers prepare to teach by writing a **lesson plan**—an organized arrangement for teaching the content for that day. Teachers write a lesson plan as an outline to guide their teaching. It should not include every word they plan to say.

There is no one right way to prepare a lesson plan. However, typical lesson plans contain these basic elements:

☐ **Topic**—a statement of the main concept to be taught. For example, "the major geographic features of the United States"

☐ **Objective**—a statement of what students will be able to do at the end of the lesson. The objective should be stated as a behavior that demonstrates an understanding of the material. For example, "On a map of the United States, students will be able to identify 80% of the major rivers, lakes, oceans, canyons, and mountain ranges."

☐ **Introduction**—something you will ask or say to gain student attention and introduce the objective. For example, "Has anyone visited the Grand Canyon? What is it like? Today you will learn about canyons and other geographic features of the United States."

☐ **Presentation**—a step-by-step outline of the procedure you will follow to teach the material. For example, you might ask students to define important terms, such as "canyon," "lake," and "mountain range" Then you might show a labeled map of the United States on an overhead projector and point out different features.

☐ **Materials**—a list of materials you need for the lesson, such as maps of different regions of the United States, some labeled and some unlabeled, plus markers to add labels.

☐ **Assessment**—a statement of how you plan to check understanding. For example, you might give a quiz or hand out an unlabeled map for students to add the correct labels.

Creating a good lesson plan is a skill developed over time through practice and experience. However, by doing this activity, you will get a taste of what lesson planning involves.

1. On a separate sheet of paper, write a brief lesson plan for elementary school students. Use the outline shown above and state the grade level for which you will prepare the plan. Choose a topic that interests you. The topic could be the arrival of the Pilgrims in America, tornadoes, or some other topic. Read information about your topic and decide what to include in your lesson.

2. Based on this activity, do you think you would enjoy a career as a school teacher? Why or why not?

_____

_____

_____

ACTIVITY—AMERICAN SIGN LANGUAGE

http://www.lifeprint.com/

American Sign Language (ASL) is communication system used by people with hearing loss. ASL uses both finger spelling and signs. In finger spelling, hand signals represent each letter of the alphabet. Other signs with the hands stand for objects and ideas. Teachers of students with hearing loss learn to communicate fluently through ASL. Using their hands, people can communicate with all the rich variety of a spoken language. Go to the Web site above to complete this activity. You could also complete the activity using a book that shows common signs in American Sign Language.

1. Click the link to "Finger spelling explanation." In the space below, sketch the finger positions required to spell your first name.

2. What is your favorite food? Use the finger spelling chart to practice spelling the name of your favorite food. Then work with a partner. Take turns finger-spelling the food name for your partner to translate. What is your partner's favorite food?

_____

3. Next click the link to "Baby's first 100 signs." Learn the signs for the seven colors demonstrated there. Practice making the sign for each color.

4. Select one color. Working with a partner, take turns making the sign for the color you selected. Try to translate your partner's color based on what you have learned from practicing the signs. Consult the Web site only if needed. What color did your partner sign?

_____

5. How are the signs for letters used in the signs for colors?

_____

_____

_____

ACTIVITY—INSTRUCTIONAL MEDIA DESIGNER

You are an instructional media designer at a planetarium. You want to design an educational program about a planet to project on the planetarium dome. You have the technologies to do still images, animations, laser lights, music, and recorded narration. Choose a planet, such as Mars or Saturn. Do library or online research to learn about the planet. Identify three facts you want to convey about this planet. Then plan a simple three-step multimedia show that teaches students these three facts. For each step in the sequence, describe the visual images, sound, and topics the narrator will cover. For example, for a show about a constellation, you might first display the stars in the constellation as brighter than those around it. You might choose calm music with a twinkling sound and have the narrator discuss where in the sky the constellation appears.

STEP 1:

Planet Fact:_____

Images:_____

Sound: _____

Narration: _____

_____

_____

STEP 2:

Planet Fact:_____

Images:_____

Sound: _____

Narration: _____

_____

_____

STEP 3:

Planet Fact:_____

Images:_____

Sound: _____

Narration: _____

_____

_____

ACTIVITY—SPECIAL NEEDS

You are a middle school teacher. Your class includes some students with special needs. **Special needs** are a wide range of challenges that make it harder for the student to learn. The special need can be a physical disability, or it can be a mental or emotional difference. As a teacher, you want to limit disruptive behavior, but you also want to address the special needs so that all your students can learn. Read the situations below and answer the questions.

Donte is a bright student. He does his homework accurately and achieves high grades on tests. However, he is withdrawn in class, especially when the lesson involves oral reading or class discussion. Donte stutters. When he speaks, other students laugh and tease him. Lately he has been avoiding the group work you assign, and his grades are beginning to suffer.

1. What is stuttering? (Do library or online research, if needed, to answer this question.)

_____

_____

_____

2. What would you do to help Donte?

_____

_____

_____

_____

To other students, Kara is known as "the brain." She finishes every class assignment well ahead of her classmates. Sometimes she intentionally does not follow directions and does assignments in her own way. Often she appears bored and cannot sit still. Her fidgeting is preventing other students from concentrating on their assignments.

3. What is Kara's "special need"?

_____

4. What would you do to help Kara?

_____

_____

_____

_____

EXPLORING A CAREER IN THE EDUCATION & TRAINING CLUSTER

The O*NET program (http://online.onetcenter.org/) is the nation's primary source of occupational information. O*NET provides data on thousands of specific jobs, including typical tasks, knowledge/skills, work styles, and education required by each. Visit the O*NET site to complete this activity. (If you do not have Internet access, gather information from your library's print version of the *Occupational Outlook Handbook*.)

1. Click the Find Occupations link. In the Quick Search box, enter a job title from the Education & Training Career Cluster that interests you. View the Details report.

(*Note:* Sample occupations in this Career Cluster can be found at the www.careerclusters.org Web site or from your teacher.)

2. Use the information you find at O*NET to fill out the following chart for the job title you chose. List the top three characteristics of the items with an asterisk (*).

Tasks*	Tools & Technology*	Knowledge*	Skills*
Abilities*	Work Activities*	Work Context*	Interests*
Work Styles*	Work Values*	Work Needs*	Related Occupations
Education Required	Median Wages	Employment	Projected Growth

3. Would you be interested in this job? Why or why not?

_____

_____

_____

ealth Science

Passions
- ☐ Working with people
- ☐ Using math, science, and technology
- ☐ Researching and investigating

Attitude
- ☐ Caring
- ☐ Sensitive

Talents
- ☐ Excellent memory
- ☐ Ability to adapt to all kinds of people
- ☐ Detail-oriented

Heart
- ☐ Likes to solve problems
- ☐ Values wellness activities

Some Career Areas to Consider
- ☐ Physical therapist's assistant
- ☐ Paramedic
- ☐ Registered nurse
- ☐ Phlebotomist
- ☐ Dietary technician

Employment Outlook
- ☐ Health care is the fastest growing industry in the United States. High demand is expected for workers in all areas of health science.
- ☐ The fastest growing occupations are home health aides, medical assistants, and physician assistants.

ACTIVITY—THERAPEUTIC SERVICES

We generally think of health care as the science of healing. Sometimes, however, people cannot be healed. **Hospice** is a special kind of care for patients whose illnesses no longer respond to cure-oriented treatment. Hospice workers focus on pain management and provide emotional support for the patients and their families. Patients who have only a few months to live can go to a hospice facility, or hospice workers will come to their homes to care for them.

For 14 years, Chris Vallandigham has worked as an administrator of Companion Hospice in Los Angeles, California. She has some moving stories to tell.

What is the main goal of the care your hospice workers provide?

The main goal of all hospice care is comfort and symptom management for anyone suffering from a terminal illness. A person with a terminal illness is defined as someone who has less than six months to live.

How does your hospice provide services?

We assign a core team of doctors, nurses, aides, counselors, physical therapists, and others to each patient and family. No one works alone. We work together to keep the patient as pain- and symptom-free as possible, 24 hours a day.

What characteristics are important for hospice workers to have?

Imagine that your mom or dad is very sick. The doctor has just told you that he or she will not live much longer, and there is nothing else that can be done. You are angry, scared, confused, and lost. What characteristics do you want in the next person who comes to see you? That is what a hospice worker must be.

What do the home health aides do?

The importance of a professional home health aide cannot be overstated. These angels provide personal care—bathing, dressing, and assisting with activities of daily living to help patients live as normally as possible. Patients often share their most personal fears and worries with the aide—even things they don't share with family. Home health aides change the lives of everyone they touch.

How do you handle the stress of caring for people who are at the end of their lives?

The stress of working in hospice can be overwhelming. This syndrome is called serial grief. We do several things to help our staff. There are monthly group counseling sessions led by a trained counselor for anyone who wants to attend. The counselor is available for private, confidential sessions for any staff member who needs help. We pray at every meeting to ask for assistance and guidance in helping our patients. This prayer also serves to remind us that we are not one, but many on a team who share the grief and the joy of all our patients. Every few months, our chaplains have a bereavement ceremony for all of us to have a time to grieve together for all who have passed through our care.

Do you sometimes fulfill special requests from your patients? What kinds?

We do look for ways to do special things for our patients. Recently, we have had a few opportunities to serve.

We met a patient with end-stage pancreatic cancer. He wanted to see the Rolling Stones in concert. Well, he was there with one of our staff, rocking out to Mick Jagger. Even his doctor thought we were crazy.

A gentleman with end-stage liver disease told us his wish. Through his life he told his family, "When I go, I want to be sitting at a slot machine in Vegas." He was and he did. His family will never forget that he truly did it his way.

Today I received a call about a patient ready to come home from the hospital. She is very sick and will die soon. She is three months old. Her mom did not think she would ever come home. Her dad is in Iraq, serving his country. Tomorrow, our staff will create a nursery complete with crib, rocking chair, decorations, clothes, and food—everything a little princess will need, so her mom only has to worry about loving and rocking her. We will call the Red Cross and whoever else will listen to try to get her dad home in time.

Who could possibly have a better job than I do?

Directions: Use the information from the article and your own experiences to answer the following questions.

1. **Specifying** What is the main goal of hospice care?

_____

_____

_____

_____

2. **Explaining** What do home health aides do for their patients?

_____

_____

_____

_____

3. **Describing** What kinds of emotions do family members feel when they learn their loved one is dying?

_____

_____

_____

_____

4. **Expressing** How did you feel when you read Chris's stories about special requests?

_____

_____

_____

_____

5. **Assessing** Based on the article, what kinds of personal characteristics does a good hospice worker need? Which of these characteristics do _you_ have?

_____

_____

_____

_____

ORGANIZING CAREER CHOICES

Directions: Choose one of the following occupations from the Health Science Cluster: physical therapist, medical lab technologist, physician assistant, or pharmacist. Then use the following table to compare and contrast it with an occupation from another Career Cluster of your choice. Finally, tell which job would suit you best. Conduct library/Internet research to locate the necessary information.

Hint: The *Occupational Outlook Handbook* (OOH) is available in most public libraries and is a good source of career information. Your school counselor's office may also have career information available. The online version of the OOH [http://www.bls.gov/oco/] is a good starting point for Internet research.

	Health Science occupation:	**Other occupation:**
Qualifications/training		
Earnings		
Employment outlook		
Working conditions		
Typical duties		
Similar occupations		
Additional sources of information about this occupation		

Which of these two jobs would suit you better? Why?

_____

_____

ACTIVITY—HEALTH INFOMATICS

Nurses work in a fast-paced world. Doctors issue orders rapidly as they move from patient to patient. An emergency room fills with patients as nurses quickly record vital data to assess patient needs. To reduce the time it takes to record information, nurses must learn a large number of abbreviations and be able to use them fluently. Medical transcriptionists must understand these abbreviations in order to translate medical notes into reports. Here is a sample.

Nurse's record:

Talia Kovak arrived at ER c/o of N&V and SOB. VS taken stat on admission. BP and HR elevated. T normal. Suspected MI. Administered O2 and IV fluids. EKG ordered. Moved to ICU.

Transcription:

Talia Kovak arrived at the emergency room complaining of nausea, vomiting, and shortness of breath. Vital signs were taken immediately on admission. Blood pressure and heart rate were elevated. Temperature was normal. A myocardial infarction [heart attack] was suspected. The nurse administered oxygen and intravenous fluids [fluids injected into a vein through a needle]. An electrocardiogram [heart function test] was ordered. The patient was moved to the intensive care unit.

Here are the abbreviations used in this sample. Write each abbreviation next to its meaning in the chart below.

BP	ER	IV	SOB
c/o	HR	MI	stat
EKG	ICU	N&V	T
		O2	VS

Abbreviation	Meaning	Abbreviation	Meaning
	heart attack		intravenous
	blood pressure		intensive care unit
	complaining of		nausea and vomiting
	temperature		electrocardiogram
	vital signs		oxygen
	emergency room		shortness of breath
	immediately		heart rate

ACTIVITY—SUPPORT SERVICES

You are a dietary technician. One of your jobs is to educate patients on how to plan nutritious meals. Today you are helping a patient learn how to evaluate food labels. This patient has osteoporosis, a disease that weakens the bones. She needs plenty of calcium in her diet while limiting sugar and saturated fat. Use this label and your knowledge of nutrition to answer the patient's questions below.

Plain Yogurt

Nutrition Facts

Serving Size 1 cup (227g)
Servings Per Container about 4

Amount per Serving

Calories 120   Calories from Fat 20

	% Daily Value*
Total Fat 2g	3%
Saturated Fat 1.5g	8%
Trans Fat 0g	
Cholesterol 10mg	3%
Sodium 150mg	6%
Total Carbohydrate 18g	6%
Dietary Fiber 3g	12%
Sugars 15g	
Protein 10g	

Vitamin A 0%	Vitamin C 0%
Calcium 40%	Iron 0%

*Percent Daily Values are based on a 2,000 calorie diet.

1. You said that plain yogurt is a good source of calcium for me. How can you tell?

_____

_____

_____

_____

_____

2. Should I eat an entire container each day to get more calcium? Please explain.

_____

_____

_____

_____

_____

_____

3. I don't like the taste of plain yogurt very much. Should I eat vanilla-flavored yogurt instead? Please explain.

_____

_____

4. What other options for flavoring should I consider? Why?

_____

_____

ACTIVITY—DIAGNOSTIC SERVICES

When you went to your doctor's office, did a nursing assistant look at a watch while holding your wrist tightly? The assistant was checking your pulse, or heart rate. This test is one way to diagnose possible heart problems.

You can check your own pulse. All you need is a watch with a second hand or a digital stop watch. Place your index and middle fingers on the inside of your wrist, below your thumb. Do you feel a beat? Look at your watch as you count the beats for 30 seconds. Multiply the result by two to determine the number of heartbeats per minute. This is your resting heart rate.

1. How many beats per minute is your resting heart rate? _____

The normal range for a resting heart rate depends on your age. Here are the normal ranges for different age groups:

Age	Beats per Minute
0-1	100-160
1-10	60-140
over 11	60-100

2. Does your resting heart rate fall within the normal range for your age?

_____

Now run in place for three minutes and take your pulse again to find your exercising heart rate.

3. What is your exercising heart rate? _____

Exercise helps to strengthen your heart and make it work more efficiently. To gain these healthy effects, however, you must exercise hard enough to make your heart work without overworking. To get the most benefit, your exercising heart rate should reach a target range of 50 to 85 percent of your maximum heart rate.

First, find your maximum heart rate. Subtract your age from 220. For example, if you are 15, you maximum heart rate is 205.

4. What is your maximum heart rate? _____

Now find your target heart rate range. Multiply your maximum heart rate by 0.5 and 0.85.

5. What is your target heart rate range? _____

6. Did your exercising heart rate fall within your target range? If not, why do you think it didn't?

_____

7. On a separate page, list five activities you could do to strengthen and improve your heart.

ACTIVITY—CODE BLUE!

Hospital workers must be prepared to handle a variety of emergencies. To make emergency response more efficient, hospitals have created a system of codes. Each code represents a specific type of emergency. When a code is called, hospital employees spring into action. They have been trained to perform specific roles in each type of emergency. For example, Code Blue is called whenever a patient goes into cardiac arrest (the heart stops). First responders know to start resuscitation and bring the "crash cart" for administering a shock to restart the heart.

Codes are not standard nationwide. Each hospital has its own system, although systems share similar codes. Below are codes developed by the Healthcare Association of Southern California.

Code	Meaning	Code	Meaning
Red	fire	Blue	adult medical emergency
White	child medical emergency	Yellow	bomb threat
Gray	combative person	Silver	person with a weapon or hostage situation
Pink	infant abduction	Purple	child abduction
Triage Internal	internal disaster	Triage External	external disaster
Orange	hazardous material spill		

1. How do codes help in emergency situations?

_____

_____

2. If the power went out throughout the hospital, what code would be called?

_____

3. Why would a power outage in a hospital be a disaster?

_____

_____

_____

4. What does the word "triage" mean? Look the word up in a dictionary if you need help.

_____

5. Why do you think "triage" is used in the code for internal and external disasters?

_____

_____

_____

ACTIVITY—TEMPORARY STAFFING

http://www.medtravelers.com/

Sometimes hospitals, clinics, or other health care facilities need extra workers on a temporary basis. The managers of these organizations know that it would be inefficient to hire and train extra workers, only to let them go when the temporary need has passed. For this reason, many health care organizations turn to medical staffing services such as Med Travelers to fill their short-term needs. Visit the Med Travelers Web site or use library resources to answer the following questions.

1. Why do you think health care facilities might have need for temporary workers?

_____

_____

_____

2. Med Travelers provides information about therapy careers and medical imaging careers. Read the descriptions of several jobs. Which do you think you would like best? Why?

_____

_____

_____

3. What are some benefits of working as a traveling temporary employee?

_____

_____

_____

4. What are some drawbacks of this kind of work?

_____

_____

_____

5. Do you think you would like working as a traveling temporary worker in the health care industry? Why or why not?

_____

_____

_____

_____

ACTIVITY—WHICH DOCTOR WILL YOU CHOOSE?

After graduating from medical school, many doctors take additional training to specialize in a particular area of medicine. At some point in your life, you may need a specialist. But what type of doctor do you need? The names of the specialists can be confusing. Sometimes the prefix—the group of letters at the beginning of the name—can provide clues to the doctor's specialty. In the chart below, write the meaning of each prefix. Use a dictionary, if needed.

Prefix	Meaning	Prefix	Meaning
1. cardio		5. maxilla	
2. derma/dermis		6. neuro	
3. gastro		7. path/patho	
4. hema/hemo		8. pod/podo	

Using what you learned about prefixes, identify the doctor you would choose from the list below for each need described in the chart. Write the name next to the need.

gastroenterologist   cardiologist
neurologist   maxillofacial surgeon
hematologist   pathologist
podiatrist   dermatologist

Physician you would choose . . .	if you . . .
9.	were having chest pain
10.	had trouble with blood clotting
11.	had nerve pain down the back of your leg
12.	had painful hammer toes
13.	wanted to treat your acne
14.	were in an accident and broke bones in your face
15.	had a tissue sample taken and needed someone to evaluate it for disease
16.	had trouble digesting food

ACTIVITY—BIOTECHNOLOGY RESEARCH AND DEVELOPMENT

People today can expect to live longer, healthier lives than did their grandparents' generation, thanks to medical research. Along with these advances, however, comes controversy. Some research methods and medical treatments involve ethical issues. **Bioethics** is the study of the ethical and moral issues related to biological research. One example is animal testing.

Medical researchers have used animals to develop vaccines against polio and measles, as well as life-saving antibiotics and cancer treatments. Operations on animals have helped develop techniques for organ transplant and open-heart surgery. Many of the medical treatments you receive have first been tested on animals. Because of animal testing, doctors can feel confident that a treatment is safe and effective before giving it to humans.

Opponents of animal testing point out that such experiments can be misleading. Animals do not respond to a drug in exactly the same way as a human will. Some opponents say that animals have as much right to life as humans. Supporters of animal testing counter by pointing out that millions of animals are killed for food each year. They believe that killing animals in research that will save human lives is no different.

1. What are some arguments in favor of using animals for medical research?

_____

_____

_____

2. What are some arguments against using animals for medical research?

_____

_____

_____

3. Where do you stand on this issue? Why?

_____

_____

_____

4. Knowing that medical research sometimes involves animal testing, would you be suited for a career as a medical researcher? Explain your answer.

_____

_____

_____

EXPLORING A CAREER IN THE HEALTH SCIENCE CLUSTER

The O*NET program (http://online.onetcenter.org/) is the nation's primary source of occupational information. O*NET provides data on thousands of specific jobs, including typical tasks, knowledge/skills, work styles, and education required by each. Visit the O*NET site to complete this activity. (If you do not have Internet access, gather information from your library's print version of the *Occupational Outlook Handbook*.)

1. Click the Find Occupations link. In the Quick Search box, enter a job title from the Health Science Career Cluster that interests you. View the Details report.

(*Note:* Sample occupations in this Career Cluster can be found at the www.careerclusters.org Web site or from your teacher.)

2. Use the information you find at O*NET to fill out the following chart for the job title you chose. List the top three characteristics of the items with an asterisk (*).

Tasks*	Tools & Technology*	Knowledge*	Skills*
Abilities*	Work Activities*	Work Context*	Interests*
Work Styles*	Work Values*	Work Needs*	Related Occupations
Education Required	Median Wages	Employment	Projected Growth

3. Would you be interested in this job? Why or why not?

_____

_____

_____

Transportation, Distribution & Logistics

Passions
- ☐ Driving or working on vehicles
- ☐ Analyzing problems
- ☐ Working with hands

Attitude
- ☐ Individualistic
- ☐ Practical

Talents
- ☐ Belief in oneself
- ☐ Detail-oriented
- ☐ Mechanical abilities

Heart
- ☐ Takes pride in accomplishments
- ☐ Is calm under pressure

Some Career Areas to Consider
- ☐ Pilot
- ☐ Logistics analyst
- ☐ Warehouse manager
- ☐ Civil engineer
- ☐ Auto mechanic

Employment Outlook
- ☐ The Bureau of Labor Statistics projects an increase in employment in this sector through 2012.
- ☐ There will be a growing number of career opportunities in a variety of professional and technical occupations as well as high-paid, entry-level occupations that can provide career advancement opportunities.

ACTIVITY—TRANSPORTATION OPERATIONS

Have you ever been at an airport and seen the air traffic controllers working in airport control towers? Air traffic controllers help maintain the flow of air traffic in a safe and orderly manner. They also help prevent aircraft collisions. Every day, air traffic controllers protect almost 2 million air passengers. In the U.S. alone, they safely direct over 60 million aircraft to their destinations each year.

More than 14,000 men and women work as air traffic controllers in the United States. Almost all of them are employed by the Federal Aviation Administration (FAA), an agency of the United States government. **Tower controllers** are probably the employees most people picture when they think of air traffic controllers. They work in glass towers managing air traffic between 3 to 30 miles from the airport. Tower controllers monitor all planes that travel through the airport's airspace. Their main job is to organize the flow of aircraft into and out of the airport.

Radar controllers watch aircraft on radar and communicate with the pilots when necessary, warning them about nearby planes, bad weather conditions, and other potential hazards. And **enroute controllers** work in more than 20 centers around the country, away from airports. They direct airplanes for most of their journey, controlling all air traffic above 17,000 feet.

There is no single path to becoming an air traffic controller. Ann Harris, a controller at Washington's National Airport, earned college degrees in Aeronautics and Air Traffic. Dale Wright of Charlotte Tower in North Carolina started his career in the military. Almost all controllers have loved airplanes since they were kids. However, loving airplanes isn't enough. The FAA requires all controllers to be at least 30 years of age and a United States citizen. Potential controllers must also pass a rigorous medical examination, including vision, hearing, and substance abuse tests.

When asked the three most important traits a good controller needs, Ann Harris responds: "Awareness, good judgment, and patience." Dale Wright cites "discipline, being a team player, and the ability to handle stress." Many controllers take great satisfaction in working with a team. And most would tell you that, although keeping America's skies safe is a huge responsibility, they wouldn't change jobs with anybody.

Directions: Use the information from the article and your own experiences to answer the following questions.

1. **Identifying** How many aircraft do air traffic controllers in the United States handle each year?

_____

_____

_____

_____

_____

2. **Contrasting** What are some differences between tower controllers and enroute controllers?

_____

_____

_____

_____

_____

3. **Naming** What are some requirements the FAA demands that air traffic controllers meet?

_____

_____

_____

_____

_____

4. **Thinking Critically** Why do you think air traffic controllers in the United States must be over 30 years old? Why must they be U.S. citizens?

_____

_____

_____

_____

_____

5. **Analyzing** Who employs most air traffic controllers in the U.S.? Why do you suppose each airport doesn't simply train and hire its own air traffic controllers?

_____

_____

_____

_____

_____

6. **Assessing** Based on the article, what kinds of personal characteristics does a good air traffic controller need? How many of these characteristics do _you_ have?

_____

_____

_____

_____

_____

ORGANIZING CAREER CHOICES

Directions: Choose one of the following occupations from the Transportation, Distribution & Logistics Cluster: bus driver, distribution manager, aerospace engineer, urban planner, safety analyst, or freight agent. Then use the following table to compare and contrast it with an occupation from another Career Cluster of your choice. Finally, tell which job would suit you best. Conduct library/Internet research to locate the necessary information.

Hint: The *Occupational Outlook Handbook* (OOH) is available in most public libraries and is a good source of career information. Your school counselor's office may also have career information available. The online version of the OOH [http://www.bls.gov/oco/] is a good starting point for Internet research.

	Transportation, Distribution & Logistics occupation:	**Other occupation:**
Qualifications/training		
Earnings		
Employment outlook		
Working conditions		
Typical duties		
Similar occupations		
Additional sources of information about this occupation		

Which of these two jobs would suit you better? Why?

_____

_____

ACTIVITY—SALES AND SERVICE

People rent automobiles for many different reasons. People most often rent a car when they travel out of town. Travelers who fly to their destinations may still want a vehicle to get around. But people rent cars for other reasons, too. For example, sometimes people who drive on a long trip rent a car to avoid putting miles on their own vehicle. And sometimes people rent cars for a few days while their own cars are being repaired. For these reasons, the car rental industry is large and growing.

1. Find some recent newspaper or magazine advertisements for car rental businesses (or search online). What kinds of vehicles and deals do they offer? Why do you think rental companies offer a variety of vehicles to their customers?

_____

_____

_____

_____

_____

2. Because so many out-of-town travelers rent vehicles, car rental businesses are natural partners with airlines. (Most rental businesses are located near airports.) Can you think of at least two other businesses that might be good partners with a car rental business?

_____

_____

_____

_____

_____

3. Suppose you operate a car rental business near a ski resort. You typically provide local maps to out-of-town customers who rent vehicles from you. What other kinds of helpful information might you provide your customers?

_____

_____

_____

_____

_____

ACTIVITY—LOGISTICS PLANNING AND MANAGEMENT

http://www.srinternational.com/

When shipping a product overseas, companies must be aware of packing, labeling, documentation, and insurance requirements. These requirements can be very complex. That is why most exporters use an international freight forwarder such as SR International Logistics to be certain the shipping requirements are met. Visit the SR International Logistics Web site to answer the following questions.

1. Read about the services provided by SR International Logistics and summarize one of them in the space below. (If you don't have Internet access, find an article about logistics in the library and summarize a service.)

_____

_____

_____

_____

2. Many logistics planners speak several different languages. Why might this be an important skill for someone who works in logistics planning? If you have Internet access, click the Team Profiles link and scan the bios of several key employees of SR International Logistics to learn more about employee qualifications for this field.

_____

_____

_____

_____

3. International trade is expected to increase in the future. How do you think this will affect employment opportunities in logistics planning?

_____

_____

_____

_____

ACTIVITY—WAREHOUSING AND DISTRIBUTION CENTER OPERATIONS

As a warehouse manager for a large book publisher, you need to hire a new shipping and receiving clerk, an entry-level job. Shipping and receiving clerks keep records of all outgoing and incoming shipments. They prepare shipping documents and mailing labels and make sure that orders have been filled correctly. Clerks must sometimes pack and carry boxes weighing up to 50 pounds. In your company, clerks use hand-held scanners to record barcodes on incoming and outgoing products to record package information on a computer. Working quickly and accurately is a big part of this job.

Today you have interviewed the following applicants for the job:

Jeremy Anderson	Emily Radner	Otis Washington
☐ High school dropout, currently working on his GED ☐ Has held three jobs in the past year; most recently worked as a forklift operator in another warehouse ☐ Hobbies include working out and surfing the Internet ☐ Arrived for interview on time ☐ Answered all of your questions in the job interview; didn't ask you any questions ☐ Tells you that he works best on his own at a slow but steady pace ☐ Tells you that he quit his last job because his supervisor "never let me finish one job before handing me another" ☐ Says that he's ready for a "fresh start" and "wants to make this happen"	☐ Recent college graduate majoring in French history ☐ Has never held a job, preferring to focus on her schoolwork ☐ Tells you she is "afraid" of computers, but seems willing to learn about them ☐ No errors on job application, but handwriting was hard to read ☐ Says she wants the job because she "loves books" ☐ Seemed friendly and excited during the interview, but could not find copies of her resume to leave with you ☐ At the end of the interview, she hands you a paper she wrote in class about the French Revolution, "to show you that I'm no dummy"	☐ Recent high school graduate; member of wrestling team and Spanish club ☐ Favorite subject in school was math ☐ Currently works two part-time jobs; juggles schedules successfully; never missed a day of work ☐ Arrived for interview on time ☐ Incorrect date was entered on job application ☐ In the interview, knew a bit about your company; asked how you got your start in warehouse operations ☐ Tells you he hopes to begin classes at a local community college within the next year ☐ Asked you to show him around the warehouse before concluding the interview

To which of these applicants will you offer the job? Explain your answer.

_____

_____

_____

_____

_____

ACTIVITY—FACILITY AND MOBILE EQUIPMENT MAINTENANCE

Do you have what it takes to be an auto mechanic? Take this quick quiz to see how much you know about the ins and outs of autos. (Your teacher has the correct answers to this test.)

1. What is "ping"?
A The noise that occurs in a vehicle when the fluid in a combustion chamber ignites because of pressure before the flame can reach it.
B The noise that occurs when the clutch has been released too quickly.
C The space between electrodes on a spark plug.
D A unit of measurement used to describe wheel alignment.

2. What is a crankshaft?
A The steel tube that connects the transmission to the rear-end housing.
B A part of a vehicle's engine that sends electricity to the ignition.
C An engine component (connected to pistons by connecting rods) that converts the up and down motion of the pistons to rotary motion used to turn the driveshaft.
D A device attached to the exhaust stack of an engine to reduce noise and increase back pressure.

3. An engine is burning oil. A dry compression test shows the cylinders to have 125 psi. A wet compression test shows 130 psi. The most likely cause of the oil burning is

A bad main bearings.
B worn piston rings.
C bad valve seals.
D bad intake manifold gasket.

4. White smoke from your car's tailpipe is caused by
A water or antifreeze entering the cylinder, and the engine trying to burn it with the fuel.
B engine oil entering the cylinder area and being burned along with the fuel air mixture.
C excess fuel that has entered the cylinder area and cannot be burned completely.
D all of the above can cause white smoke.

5. What color is fresh automatic transmission fluid?
A black
B red
C green
D clear

6. The rear tires of a front-wheel-drive car have a series of "cups" worn into them. The most likely cause is
A binding rear brakes.
B the rear camber is out of adjustment.
C a stuck parking brake cable.
D bad rear shock absorbers.

What kinds of personal characteristics does a good auto mechanic need? How many of these characteristics do *you* have?

_____

_____

_____

_____

ACTIVITY—HEALTH, SAFETY, AND ENVIRONMENTAL MANAGEMENT

Employees in the Health and Safety Management field assess safety risks and help businesses manage them. For example, safety engineers study industrial processes and the way people behave to anticipate and reduce the chances of an accident happening. They must also be familiar with health and safety laws and regulations.

Many companies provide information for employees to help keep them safe at work. Do some library or Internet research about basic on-the-job safety tips. (Use the *Readers' Guide to Periodical Literature* or search online using the keywords *workplace safety*.) The Occupational Safety and Health (OSHA) Web site (www.osha.gov) and publications may also provide you with valuable information.

Record your findings in the space below. (Two tips have been given to get you started.) Then use the information you have found to create a safety brochure to distribute to employees at your small office. You may create your brochure by hand on a separate sheet of paper or on a computer program. Feel free to add any artwork or design elements you think would help promote employee safety.

Workplace Safety Tips

☐ Avoid leaving cords across walkways or file cabinet drawers open

☐ Fill drawers and shelves from the bottom up, by allowing the weight to keep them from tipping over

ACTIVITY—TRANSPORTATION SYSTEMS/INFRASTRUCTURE PLANNING, MANAGEMENT AND REGULATION

Many American highways have become too crowded. It is not hard to understand why. From 1950 – 1986, the U.S. population increased by 60 percent. But the number of vehicles increased by almost 260 percent! And fewer highways and roads were built during this time. In Los Angeles, rush-hour traffic on the freeway moves along at only 35 miles per hour. If the situation is not fixed, experts believe that traffic will move at only 11 miles per hour by 2010. **Traffic engineers** can help reduce congestion by studying traffic patterns and rerouting traffic when needed.

1. Identify an intersection or stretch of road in your community with a traffic flow problem. Visit this location and, from a safe distance, record the number of vehicles that pass in 15 minutes. Repeat your count on two other days, at different times. Then enter all of your information in the chart below.

Location of observation:	
Date and time	*Number of vehicles observed*

2. If you were a traffic engineer, how often do you think you would need to repeat your count to get an accurate idea of traffic flow? Explain.

_____

_____

_____

_____

3. What kinds of technology could traffic engineers use to measure traffic flow? Do some library or Internet research on technology such as the Intelligent Vehicle Highway System (IVHS) and other systems. Add your own ideas as well. Report your findings below.

_____

_____

_____

_____

_____

ACTIVITY—TRANSPORTATION OPERATIONS

You are a long-distance truck driver. Today you are hauling a shipment from Indianapolis, Indiana to Norfolk, Virginia. Before you leave on your trip, you will need to inspect your vehicle for safety. Use library or Internet resources to list some things you should check before you get on the road.

_____

_____

_____

_____

Now find a road atlas in the library or an online mapping service such as MapQuest and use it to record detailed directions from Indianapolis to Norfolk. Your journey begins on East Washington Street in Indianapolis and ends on East City Hall Avenue in Norfolk.

For each step along the way, record the name of the road you will use and the general direction you will be traveling. When you need to turn onto a different road, indicate the correct exit number. Also record the approximate mileage from one step to the next.

You can plan on driving 50 miles for every hour on your trip. Your company allows you to be on the road for only 8 hours each day, so you may need to find a motel to spend the night. Determine approximately where you are likely to be after 8 hours of travel, then use library or Internet resources to locate a place to stay. Record that on your list of directions also.

_____

_____

_____

_____

_____

Finally, use library or Internet resources to find some ways satellites and Global Positioning Systems (GPS) are changing the ways truck drivers work.

_____

_____

_____

_____

EXPLORING A CAREER IN THE TRANSPORTATION, DISTRIBUTION & LOGISTICS CLUSTER

The O*NET program (http://online.onetcenter.org/) is the nation's primary source of occupational information. O*NET provides data on thousands of specific jobs, including typical tasks, knowledge/skills, work styles, and education required by each. Visit the O*NET site to complete this activity. (If you do not have Internet access, gather information from your library's print version of the *Occupational Outlook Handbook*.)

1. Click the Find Occupations link. In the Quick Search box, enter a job title from the Transportation, Distribution & Logistics Career Cluster that interests you. View the Details report.

(*Note:* Sample occupations in this Career Cluster can be found at the www.careerclusters.org Web site or from your teacher.)

2. Use the information you find at O*NET to fill out the following chart for the job title you chose. List the top three characteristics of the items with an asterisk (*).

Tasks*	Tools & Technology*	Knowledge*	Skills*
Abilities*	Work Activities*	Work Context*	Interests*
Work Styles*	Work Values*	Work Needs*	Related Occupations
Education Required	Median Wages	Employment	Projected Growth

3. Would you be interested in this job? Why or why not?

_____

_____

_____

Passions

- ☐ Working with hands
- ☐ Designing or building
- ☐ Working with tools

Attitude

- ☐ Self-motivated
- ☐ Detail-oriented

Talents

- ☐ Mechanical ability
- ☐ Math and science ability
- ☐ Thinking skills

Heart

- ☐ Likes to work with people
- ☐ Needs standards and rules

Some Career Areas to Consider

- ☐ Electrician
- ☐ Contractor
- ☐ Architect
- ☐ Highway worker
- ☐ Environmental engineer

Employment Outlook

- ☐ The Architecture & Construction Cluster is one of the largest in the United States, accounting for almost 14 million jobs.
- ☐ Opportunities are expected to be especially good in the construction industry, due in part to the shortage of qualified workers. Earnings in construction are significantly higher than the average for all industries.

ACTIVITY—DESIGN/PRE-CONSTRUCTION

More and more Americans are moving away from cities and even suburbs into rural areas. It has been estimated that more than 300 acres of countryside are lost every hour due to land development. The spread of an urban or suburban area into nearby countryside is called **urban sprawl**.

Many urban planners believe that sprawl is bad. They point to such problems as increased air and water pollution; higher energy use for homes and transportation; the loss of farmland and wild areas; and a need to increase road building so residents can drive to their jobs, which are usually miles away. Instead of sprawl, these planners have begun to promote what they call **smart growth**.

The smart growth concept focuses on the long-term effects of land development. Smart growth strategies promote development while preserving natural resources. Planners design smart growth communities with attractive sidewalks to allow pedestrian traffic; a town center served by busses, streetcars, and other mass transit; and a mix of housing alternatives such as private homes and apartments. The goal is to save open space, reduce auto dependence, and strengthen community ties.

Smart growth advocates often must work with diverse groups—all of whom want different things—to find solutions. Fortunately, they have had many successes. For example, city planners in Rutland, Vermont, worked with company officials from Wal-Mart to locate a new store in an abandoned building near the city's downtown area. This saved the company money (it did not need to build a new store) and preserved acres of countryside.

Near Dallas, Texas, planners in the town of Addison worked with developers to create a compact community called Addison Circle. This pedestrian-friendly community is a diverse mixture of homes, offices, retail shops, and parks—all within walking distance of one another. It has attracted residents and businesses that would probably have gobbled up countryside around Dallas.

Working together, urban planners and developers have proven that urban sprawl can be controlled. But there is always room for more good ideas.

Directions: Use the information from the article and your own experiences to answer the following questions.

1. **Defining** What is urban sprawl?

_____

_____

_____

_____

_____

2. **Identifying** What are some common problems associated with urban sprawl?

_____

_____

_____

_____

_____

3. **Explaining** How does smart growth try to reduce the impact of urban sprawl?

_____

_____

_____

_____

_____

4. **Making Connections** One goal of smart growth is to strengthen community ties. How might you feel more connected to your community if you walked to the store or to work, as opposed to driving everywhere?

_____

_____

_____

_____

_____

5. **Comparing** Would you like to live in a smart growth community? How might it be different to live in a smart growth community than where you live now?

_____

_____

_____

_____

_____

6. **Assessing** Based on the article, what kinds of personal characteristics does a good urban planner need? How many of these characteristics do _you_ have?

_____

_____

_____

_____

_____

ORGANIZING CAREER CHOICES

Directions: Choose one of the following occupations from the Architecture & Construction Cluster: surveyor, safety director, electrician, or millwright. Then use the following table to compare and contrast it with an occupation from another Career Cluster of your choice. Finally, tell which job would suit you best. Conduct library/Internet research to locate the necessary information.

Hint: The *Occupational Outlook Handbook* (OOH) is available in most public libraries and is a good source of career information. Your school counselor's office may also have career information available. The online version of the OOH [http://www.bls.gov/oco/] is a good starting point for Internet research.

	Architecture & Construction occupation:	**Other occupation:**
Qualifications/training		
Earnings		
Employment outlook		
Working conditions		
Typical duties		
Similar occupations		
Additional sources of information about this occupation		

Which of these two jobs would suit you better? Why?

_____

_____

ACTIVITY—DESIGN/PRE-CONSTRUCTION

Landscape designers plan the arrangements of trees, bushes, and gardens for homes and offices. In this exercise, you are going to create a design for a small garden in front of your home or school. You will sketch the area you plan to use for the garden, then indicate which plants you want to grow.

Before you begin, do some library or Internet research on basic landscape design (keywords *landscape design*). You will also want to do some research to find out what kinds of plants grow well in your region, and if you need shade-loving or sun-loving plants. (You'll need to check out the site of your proposed garden to find out!)

1. In the space below, write the basic steps in developing a landscape design. Use the information from your research to help you.

_____

_____

_____

_____

2. Use the following space to write some common mistakes people make when they plan a garden.

_____

_____

_____

_____

3. Now write the names of some plants you think would work well in your garden. Are there any plants you need to avoid?

_____

_____

_____

_____

4. Finally, use a separate sheet of paper (or a computer program) to draw your design. Indicate the size of your garden and the name, color, and location of each plant.

ACTIVITY—CONSTRUCTION

People who work in construction need to know how much material they will need to complete a job. For example, if a roofer is going to put new shingles on the roof of your home, she will need to know the area of the roof. Then she will know how many shingles to buy.

In this exercise, you will brush up on your calculating skills. First, use the space below to record the formulas needed to make the calculations shown. (You might remember the formulas from your math courses. If not, use library or Internet research to find them.) Then answer the questions that follow.

Area of a square: _____   Perimeter of a square: _____

Area of a rectangle: _____   Perimeter of a rectangle: _____

Area of a circle: _____

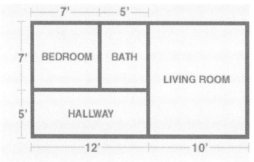

1. What is the perimeter of the above floor plan?

_____

2. Suppose you want to put carpet on the floor of the living room shown above. How many square feet of carpet will you need?

_____

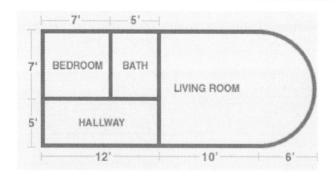

3. Suppose your living room is shaped as above. Now how many square feet of carpet will you need?

_____

ACTIVITY—DESIGN/PRE-CONSTRUCTION

Have you ever seen a picture of the Brown Derby Restaurant in Los Angeles? It is shaped like an actual derby hat. How about the home office of the Longaberger Company in Newark, Ohio? The building of this basketmaking firm is in the form of a giant basket. And then there's the Big Duck, a building for a poultry store designed in the shape of a giant duck.

These are all examples of "novelty" architecture. Novelty architecture (also called programmatic or mimetic architecture) is distinguished by buildings that look like animals, people, or household objects. Many of these buildings were built to advertise the products sold inside. Novelty architecture was especially popular in the 1930s. Coffee shops were built in the shape of big coffee pots; fruit stands were shaped like giant oranges; and hot dog stands . . . well, you guessed it.

In this activity, you are going to sketch a novelty building that you might enjoy seeing in your community. Before getting to work, use library/Internet resources to check out these examples (or find your own using search words *novelty architecture*):

- ☐ Brown Derby Restaurant, Los Angeles, CA
- ☐ Benewah Milk Bottle, Spokane, WA
- ☐ Bondurant's Pharmacy, Lexington, KY
- ☐ The Conga Room, Los Angeles, CA
- ☐ Richmond Dairy Apartments, Richmond, VA
- ☐ The Donut Hole, La Puente, CA
- ☐ The Longaberger Company, Newark, OH

- ☐ Salvador's Ice Cream, S. Dartmouth, MA
- ☐ The Haines Shoe House, York County, PA
- ☐ Tea Pot Dome service station, Zillah, WA
- ☐ Wigwam Motel, Holbrook, AZ
- ☐ The Big Duck, Long Island, NY
- ☐ The Tractor, Turlock, CA

Now use a separate sheet of paper—or a computer program—to create a drawing of your own novelty building. You can design a building to advertise a local product or business; or you can design a building just for fun. Think of a store in your community that might operate out of a novelty building. Or perhaps your area is famous for something: a certain type of food, or sports team, or natural attraction. Maybe your building could advertise that. Use your imagination.

ACTIVITY—CONSTRUCTION

Switches open and close electrical circuits, allowing power to flow through lights and appliances. The most familiar switch, often referred to by do-it-yourselfers as a "light switch" is actually called a "single pole switch." With this type of switch, flipping the lever up completes the circuit, turning on the lights or appliances. Flipping the lever down breaks the circuit, turning off the power.

In the space below, or on a separate sheet of paper, write the directions for replacing a simple single pole switch. Also include a diagram of the switch, clearly showing the proper wires and their connections to the switch.

Use library/Internet resources to help you determine the proper steps to follow to replace the switch.

Based on this exercise, do you think you would enjoy a career as an electrician? Explain.

_____

_____

_____

_____

ACTIVITY—MAINTENANCE/OPERATIONS

http://www.implosionworld.com/

You've probably seen videos of a large building or sports stadium being brought down by explosives. The people responsible for such operations are called **demolition engineers**. It always looks impressive to see a large skyscraper crumble into itself in just a matter of moments. But demolition engineers really need to know what they are doing. Imploding a building requires precise and careful planning. Demolition engineers must place the explosives properly for maximum effect. They use their understanding of physics to collapse the structure safely.

Do some library or Internet research on the work of demolition engineers (use keywords like *explosive demolition* or *building implosion* or visit the implosionworld.com Web site). Then answer the following questions.

1. How do explosive demolition techniques use gravity to bring down structures?

_____

_____

_____

_____

_____

2. Briefly explain how demolition engineers use 3-D computer models in their work.

_____

_____

_____

_____

_____

3. Do you think you would enjoy working as a demolition engineer? Why or why not?

_____

_____

_____

_____

ACTIVITY—WHAT'S IN YOUR TOOL BELT?

Do you know the difference between an awl and a push-pull drill? Do you know which tool to use to get the job done right? To find out, match the name of the construction tool below to its description. (Your teacher has the correct answers to this test.)

☐ auger
☐ caliper
☐ chisel
☐ crosscut saw
☐ hacksaw

☐ level
☐ screwdriver
☐ trowel
☐ vise
☐ wrench

Name of Tool	Description
1.	Used for metal cutting.
2.	Used to spread mortar or concrete or to apply flooring glue.
3.	Used to make cuts in wood that can't be made with a saw or plane.
4.	Used to measure inside and outside diameters.
5.	Used to hold or twist a nut or bolt.
6.	Used for wood cutting.
7.	Used to tighten screws.
8.	Used to bore holes through materials.
9.	Used to measure if a piece of material is horizontal or vertical.
10.	Used to hold materials steady for sawing or sanding.

Based on how well you did on this quiz, do you think you would enjoy working in construction? Why or why not?

_____

_____

_____

_____

ACTIVITY—MAINTENANCE/OPERATIONS

Highway maintenance work is very dangerous. Between 1989 and 1998, more than 7,000 people (workers as well as drivers) lost their lives in U.S. highway work zones. Traffic is sometimes as close as one or two feet from the people who are performing highway maintenance.

Accidents involving highway workers occur for many reasons. Sometimes there are not enough signs alerting drivers that road work is happening. Traffic noise makes it difficult for workers to hear shouted warnings or the movement of large pieces of equipment. And there is often no place for workers to escape for protection once a vehicle crosses the barriers of a work zone.

In this exercise, you will do some library/Internet research on highway worker safety and answer some questions. Then you will generate one idea that might make life safer for the men and women who work along our nation's highways.

1. What is the number one cause of accidents in highway work zones?

_____

_____

2. How much longer does it take to drive through a two-mile work zone at 45 mph instead of at 65 mph?

_____

_____

3. The state of Michigan has tried to protect highway workers by increasing the penalties for drivers who injure or kill a highway worker. Describe one other plan or program you read about in your research that is designed to protect highway workers.

_____

_____

_____

_____

_____

4. On a separate sheet of paper, write about an idea you think would help protect highway workers. For example, it could be a new law, a safety awareness program, better signs or lighting, or a crash-protection device. Explain how your idea would work and why you think it might help.

EXPLORING A CAREER IN THE ARCHITECTURE & CONSTRUCTION CLUSTER

The O*NET program (http://online.onetcenter.org/) is the nation's primary source of occupational information. O*NET provides data on thousands of specific jobs, including typical tasks, knowledge/skills, work styles, and education required by each. Visit the O*NET site to complete this activity. (If you do not have Internet access, gather information from your library's print version of the *Occupational Outlook Handbook*.)

1. Click the Find Occupations link. In the Quick Search box, enter a job title from the Architecture & Construction Career Cluster that interests you. View the Details report.

(*Note:* Sample occupations in this Career Cluster can be found at the www.careerclusters.org Web site or from your teacher.)

2. Use the information you find at O*NET to fill out the following chart for the job title you chose. List the top three characteristics of the items with an asterisk (*).

Tasks*	Tools & Technology*	Knowledge*	Skills*
Abilities*	Work Activities*	Work Context*	Interests*
Work Styles*	Work Values*	Work Needs*	Related Occupations
Education Required	Median Wages	Employment	Projected Growth

3. Would you be interested in this job? Why or why not?

_____

_____

_____

Name _____

Date _____

Passions
- ☐ Putting things together
- ☐ Repairing equipment
- ☐ Making decisions

Attitude
- ☐ Precise
- ☐ Logical

Talents
- ☐ Problem-solving ability
- ☐ Math, science, and technology ability
- ☐ Ability to imagine a final product

Heart
- ☐ Likes to work with hands
- ☐ Likes to be accurate

Some Career Areas to Consider
- ☐ Production engineer
- ☐ Welder
- ☐ Lab technician
- ☐ Safety engineer
- ☐ Machinist

Employment Outlook
- ☐ Manufacturing employment is expected to increase slightly due to strong demand for high-tech electrical goods and pharmaceuticals.
- ☐ Jobs in this Cluster will be most plentiful in logistics/inventory and maintenance, installation, and repair.

ACTIVITY—QUALITY ASSURANCE

W. Edwards Deming was born in Sioux City, Iowa in 1900. By the late 1920s, he had received his PhD. in mathematics from Yale University. He began working on ways to improve manufacturing production using statistical control methods. He developed a technique to measure quality by examining random samples of the manufactured product. The samples were tested and compared to specific standards to make sure they met customers' expectations. If they didn't, the manufacturer would take steps to fix the problem.

After World War II, Deming's statistical control methods became popular in Japan. Japanese companies learned that statistical control improved product quality, reduced expenses, and increased productivity. After Japanese manufacturers began applying Deming's techniques, they began seeing an increased demand for their products—not only in Japan, but around the world. In particular, Japanese automakers used Deming's ideas to improve product quality and lower costs to create worldwide demand.

Deming also developed a model for quality control called the Deming Cycle. It involves a series of four repetitive steps for continuous improvement and learning:

☐ *Plan*: plan ahead for change; predict/analyze the results
☐ *Do*: carry out the plan
☐ *Check*: study the results
☐ *Act*: take action to standardize or improve the results

Companies in the United States did not show much interest in Deming's ideas until the 1980s. Today, statistical quality control is practiced all around the world.

Directions: Use the information from the article and your own experiences to answer the following questions.

1. **Explaining** Briefly explain how Deming's statistical control procedures work.

_____

_____

_____

_____

_____

2. **Listing** What three benefits did Japanese manufacturers find when they began using Deming's statistical control procedures?

_____

_____

_____

_____

_____

3. **Identifying** What are the four steps of the Deming Cycle?

_____

_____

_____

_____

_____

4. **Evaluating** When you think of the "the best automobile," which model comes to mind? How do you think it benefits that company to be known for producing high quality products?

_____

_____

_____

_____

_____

5. **Analyzing** Suppose you use the Deming Cycle to develop a study procedure for this class. Your goal is to get better grades on tests. What could you do to perform the *Check* step of the cycle?

_____

_____

_____

_____

_____

6. **Assessing** What kinds of personal characteristics do you think a good quality control technician needs? How many of these characteristics do *you* have?

_____

_____

_____

_____

_____

ORGANIZING CAREER CHOICES

Directions: Choose one of the following occupations from the Manufacturing Cluster: tool and die maker, precision inspector, laser systems technician, environmental engineer, or material handler. Then use the following table to compare and contrast it with an occupation from another Career Cluster of your choice. Finally, tell which job would suit you best. Conduct library/Internet research to locate the necessary information.

Hint: The *Occupational Outlook Handbook* (OOH) is available in most public libraries and is a good source of career information. Your school counselor's office may also have career information available. The online version of the OOH [http://www.bls.gov/oco/] is a good starting point for Internet research.

	Manufacturing occupation:	**Other occupation:**
Qualifications/training		
Earnings		
Employment outlook		
Working conditions		
Typical duties		
Similar occupations		
Additional sources of information about this occupation		

Which of these two jobs would suit you better? Why?

_____

_____

ACTIVITY—PRODUCTION

Everyone has studied famous American inventors like Thomas Edison and Alexander Graham Bell. Inventions such as the electric light bulb, the telephone, and the airplane have changed the world. But have you ever heard of the No-Rope Jump Rope, the Electrical Nuisance Preventer, or the Skateboard Pirate? Probably not.

Every product you buy had to be invented and designed first. And every year, thousands of people invent all sorts of strange devices. Most of them, like the Mechanical Clothespin, never get off the drawing board. But then again, the personal computer probably seemed like a crazy idea long, long ago.

Use library/Internet resources to find out more about strange inventions. (**Hint:** Try using keywords like *strange inventions* or *weird inventions* in your search. Also check to see if your library has a book called *World's Wackiest Inventions* by A.E. Brown and H.A. Jeffcott.) Then answer the following questions.

1. What was the most unusual invention you found? Describe it and briefly explain how it was supposed to have been made.

_____

_____

_____

_____

_____

_____

2. If you had the right materials, do you think you could actually put together the item you described in question 1? Why or why not?

_____

_____

_____

_____

_____

3. On a separate sheet of paper, design your own "wacky" invention. Make a drawing or model you could use to show someone how to manufacture the item, and write one paragraph explaining how to use it.

ACTIVITY— MANUFACTURING PRODUCTION PROCESS DEVELOPMENT

http://www.ic3d.com/index.html

Mass customization allows companies to provide goods to customers tailored to their personal tastes. One such company, Interactive Custom Clothes Company, designs, manufactures, and sells clothes customized to the personal requirements of its patrons. Visit the company's Web site—and do some additional library/Internet research about other mass customizers—to answer the following questions.

1. What kinds of products are being manufactured and sold by mass customizers?

_____

_____

2. What are some advantages for the customer who uses mass customization? For the producer?

_____

_____

3. Pick a product you might order from a mass customizer—like a pair of jeans, a bicycle, or a pair of shoes—and describe it exactly the way you would want it in the space below.

_____

_____

_____

4. Now tell how much more you would be willing to pay for the item you described in question 3, as compared to a "regular" item you might buy at the shopping mall.

_____

_____

_____

5. Do you think mass customization of clothing will become more or less popular in the next ten years? Explain your answer.

_____

_____

_____

ACTIVITY—QUALITY ASSURANCE

The Snuggle Sock Company manufactures and sells a wide variety of socks for women. The company's latest design—a brightly colored line of socks called Neon Toes—is generating a lot of customer complaints. It seems that, after two or three washes, the socks no longer hold their color. There have also been complaints about the colors "running" during washing, staining customers' other clothes. As a quality control expert, you have been asked to find some ways the company might prevent these problems from occurring.

1. Use library/Internet research to find some steps the company might take to prevent the colors from fading and running. Use search keywords such as *dyeing process* or *dyeing fabric* to start your research.

Ask yourself: What kind of material (like cotton) would be best to use for the socks? What kinds of dyes should be used? Could anything be added to the dyes to make them more colorfast? Report your findings here.

_____

_____

_____

_____

2. Consider some other alternatives. Could you add some instructions to the product packaging telling customers how to wash their socks to minimize color fading and running? Write some instructions below.

_____

_____

_____

_____

3. On a separate sheet of paper, write three paragraphs summarizing possible solutions and recommending one.

4. Based on this exercise, do you think you would enjoy a career in quality assurance? Explain.

_____

_____

_____

_____

ACTIVITY—LOGISTICS AND INVENTORY CONTROL

When a business "takes inventory," it determines the number and value of the products it has on hand by counting or weighing them. Businesses must always be aware of the merchandise they have on hand. Good inventory control helps businesses control theft and reorder efficiently. It also helps businesses keep track of the dollar value of their inventory.

Many large businesses maintain a **perpetual inventory** system. At a large grocery store, for example, items might be recorded into inventory on a computer when they are delivered to the store. When someone buys the item, a scanning system at the checkout line subtracts it from inventory. But businesses still sometimes need to count their merchandise by hand.

1. Ted's Sporting Goods has been having a problem with shoplifting. Use library/Internet resources to research some ways inventory control might help this business deal with this problem.

_____

_____

_____

_____

2. Take your own personal inventory of something you own. For example, you could count the number of CDs you own, the number of books in your home, or the number of clothes hanging in your closet. Record your results below.

_____

_____

_____

_____

3. Can you find at least two ways to organize the items you counted in step 2? For example, you might organize your CDs in alphabetical order; or by type of music; or from most favorite to least favorite.

_____

_____

_____

_____

_____

ACTIVITY—MAINTENANCE, INSTALLATION, AND REPAIR

Do you think you know computers inside-out? Are you interested in a career maintaining and repairing computers? Take this quick test to find out how much you really know about troubleshooting computer problems. (Your teacher has the correct answers to this test.)

1. The best choice for a specification for a video card would be
A AGP.
B CAS.
C CPU.
D CMYK.

2. EIDE cables connect to
A the processor.
B the hard disk.
C the video card.
D the sound card.

3. To computer technicians, UPS stands for
A Universal Power Supply.
B Uniform Programming Service.
C Uninterruptable Power Supply.
D Unit Ping Size.

4. The spec for the holes in a monitor's aperture grill is called
A dot pitch.
B aperture holes.
C grill holes.
D CRT.

5. The primary threat from a buildup of dust inside a computer is
A heat buildup.
B computer virus.
C short circuit.
D loss of sound.

6. Which of the following would usually *not* be found on a motherboard?
A PCI bus
B CPU
C IDE controller
D power supply unit

Based on how well you did on this quiz, do you think you would make a good computer technician? Why or why not?

_____

_____

_____

_____

ACTIVITY—MANUFACTURING PRODUCTION PROCESS DEVELOPMENT

Employees in Manufacturing Production Process Development are responsible for product design and design of the manufacturing process. They work with customers to make sure the manufacturing process produces a product that customers are happy with. One of their most important jobs is developing packaging that protects the product until consumers buy it and take it home.

In this exercise, you and a partner will take on the roles of design engineers at the local potato chip factory. You will work together to construct a container that will protect a single potato chip, which you will carry in your backpack for three days. You should try to design the smallest, lightest package possible. Large, bulky packages will just add to the cost of the product—and management doesn't want that!

Before you begin, review these rules:

- ☐ Use materials of your choosing to create your package. For example, you could create your package from a cut-up tissue box.
- ☐ Use only one potato chip for the experiment. You cannot change the potato chip in any way. (For example, you cannot coat it with petroleum jelly to absorb shock.) You must be able to eat the chip when you remove it from the package.

1. Discuss with your partner some possible materials you could use to construct your package. Then work together to design and construct the package.

2. After you have built your package and safely sealed the chip inside, decide who will carry the package. Place it in your backpack and leave it there for three days.

3. After the three days are up, remove the container. Is the chip still whole?

_____

4. Compare your package with your classmates' creations. How much did your package weigh? Suppose one ounce of packaging material costs $5. How much did your package cost?

_____

5. Whose structure successfully protected the chip for the least amount of money?

_____

ACTIVITY—HEALTH, SAFETY, AND ENVIRONMENTAL ASSURANCE

A **hazard** is any activity, situation, or substance that can cause harm. The two main kinds of hazards are health hazards and safety hazards. Examples of health hazards include chemical (cleaning products), biological (bacteria, dust), or physical (electric currents, heat). Safety hazards include slipping/tripping hazards, moving machinery parts, and fire hazards.

In this exercise, you are going to explore your classroom (or, with your teacher's permission, a larger area of your school) for possible hazards and record them on a worksheet.

1. First, do some library/Internet research on workplace and classroom hazards. Make a list of commonly found hazards and some safety questions to keep in mind when inspecting a site for hazards.

_____

_____

_____

_____

_____

_____

2. Now take 15 minutes to search your classroom/school area to identify potential hazards in the following categories. Also suggest a way to eliminate each hazard you find.

Physical space
- ☐ Floors
- ☐ Walls
- ☐ Ceilings
- ☐ Doors
- ☐ Windows
- ☐ Furniture
- ☐ Equipment

Environment
- ☐ Lighting
- ☐ Air quality
- ☐ Temperature
- ☐ Noise
- ☐ Electrical
- ☐ Chemical
- ☐ Biological

Report your findings to your teacher on a separate sheet of paper.

3. Finally, name one hazard you face every day at home or on your way to/from school. Tell how you might remove or reduce that hazard.

_____

_____

_____

EXPLORING A CAREER IN THE MANUFACTURING CLUSTER

The O*NET program (http://online.onetcenter.org/) is the nation's primary source of occupational information. O*NET provides data on thousands of specific jobs, including typical tasks, knowledge/skills, work styles, and education required by each. Visit the O*NET site to complete this activity. (If you do not have Internet access, gather information from your library's print version of the *Occupational Outlook Handbook*.)

1. Click the Find Occupations link. In the Quick Search box, enter a job title from the Manufacturing Career Cluster that interests you. View the Details report.

(*Note:* Sample occupations in this Career Cluster can be found at the www.careerclusters.org Web site or from your teacher.)

2. Use the information you find at O*NET to fill out the following chart for the job title you chose. List the top three characteristics of the items with an asterisk (*).

Tasks*	Tools & Technology*	Knowledge*	Skills*
Abilities*	Work Activities*	Work Context*	Interests*
Work Styles*	Work Values*	Work Needs*	Related Occupations
Education Required	Median Wages	Employment	Projected Growth

3. Would you be interested in this job? Why or why not?

_____

_____

_____

Science, Technology, Engineering & Mathematics

Passions
- ☐ Building and repairing things
- ☐ Working with tools
- ☐ Working with hands

Attitude
- ☐ Curious
- ☐ Quiet

Talents
- ☐ Math/science/technology ability
- ☐ Problem-solving ability
- ☐ Mechanical ability

Heart
- ☐ Likes to work alone
- ☐ Likes to investigate the "why" of things

Some Career Areas to Consider
- ☐ Biotechnology lab assistant
- ☐ Crime scene analyst
- ☐ Astronomer
- ☐ Metallurgist
- ☐ Economist

Employment Outlook
- ☐ Greater awareness of environmental and public health problems will increase the demand for scientists, technologists, and engineers to develop solutions.
- ☐ There will also be a growing emphasis toward preventing problems rather than simply controlling those that already exist.

ACTIVITY—SCIENCE AND MATHEMATICS

The U.S. Department of Labor expects the field of statistics to grow even faster than computer science. Statisticians analyze all sorts of data, often to make predictions about how people will behave or what events are likely to occur. Special statisticians called **actuaries** crunch numbers and use computer spreadsheets, databases, and statistical analysis software. They study uncertain future events, especially those of interest to insurance companies and pension programs.

For more than 15 years, Mary Kenkel has worked as an actuary for a large management consulting firm in Cincinnati, Ohio. She gives us an idea of what her work is like:

Mary, how did you decide to become an actuary?

I heard about the actuarial field from my cousin, who is an insurance actuary. It sounded like it might be a good fit since it requires a lot of math/statistics work. Frankly, I also found out that the pay can be rewarding.

What kind of training and education did you receive to prepare for your career as an actuary?

My math degree was the only relevant education that I had going into the job. But once I started my career, I was required to receive certification as an actuary. This certification can be on multiple levels. Each level requires a series of rather grueling exams. The entire process can take anywhere from 5 to 10 years.

What's the best part of your job?

Probably the best part is what we term "special projects." This is the work that is outside my usual duties. It can be anything different—plan mergers and acquisitions, or plan design, in which a company is changing the structure of its employee benefit program. These types of jobs are typically very hard work and are usually on a very tight deadline, but the work is much more interesting than usual.

What are three important characteristics that you believe an actuary needs?

*You have to be **very** detail-oriented. And you have to be good with people. There's a lot of client contact and clients are often unreasonably demanding and difficult. You have to be able to handle that.*

Frankly, it's also good to have a rather high threshold for repetition. You'll do the same thing over and over again, year after year.

In your experience, is this a profession in which both men and women can be successful?

Absolutely. Probably 50 percent of the actuaries I know are women.

What are some possible career paths in your field?

The actuarial profession has two main career paths. You can work in consulting, like I did, which means that you'll work with companies to develop and value their employee benefit packages, pension plans, and things like that. Or, you could work for an insurance company setting rates for benefit plans, typically medical plans.

The general consensus among consulting actuaries whom I know is that consulting is the more well-paid and interesting way to go.

Directions: Use the information from the article and your own experiences to answer the following questions.

1. **Explaining** What kinds of work do actuaries perform?

_____

_____

_____

_____

_____

2. **Identifying** Besides mathematics, name two other courses you might take that would help you prepare for an actuarial career.

_____

_____

_____

_____

_____

3. **Hypothesizing** The population of the United States is getting older. How might this affect the demand for actuaries?

_____

_____

_____

_____

_____

4. **Making Inferences** Do you suppose that actuaries are well paid? How do you know?

_____

_____

_____

_____

_____

5. **Assessing** Based on the article, what kinds of personal characteristics does a good actuary need? How many of these characteristics do _you_ have?

_____

_____

_____

_____

_____

ORGANIZING CAREER CHOICES

Directions: Choose one of the following occupations from the Science, Technology, Engineering & Mathematics Cluster: drafter, architectural engineer, mathematician, toxicologist, or oceanographer. Then use the following table to compare and contrast it with an occupation from another Career Cluster of your choice. Finally, tell which job would suit you best. Conduct library/Internet research to locate the necessary information.

Hint: The *Occupational Outlook Handbook* (OOH) is available in most public libraries and is a good source of career information. Your school counselor's office may also have career information available. The online version of the OOH [http://www.bls.gov/oco/] is a good starting point for Internet research.

	Science, Technology, Engineering & Mathematics occupation:	Other occupation:
Qualifications/training		
Earnings		
Employment outlook		
Working conditions		
Typical duties		
Similar occupations		
Additional sources of information about this occupation		

Which of these two jobs would suit you better? Why?

_____

_____

ACTIVITY—ENGINEERING AND TECHNOLOGY

Civil engineers know that the shape and structure of a substance can change its strength. Some shapes and structures can support more weight than others.

Do you think a sheet of paper can support the weight of a heavy book? The answer is yes: *if* you first change the paper's shape by folding, rolling, or bending it. In this activity you will work with some classmates to build a portable structure out of paper and tape that will support the weight of a book.

First, your teacher will need to divide the class into teams of four or five students. Each team will need:

- ☐ 25 sheets of notebook paper (each team member will contribute five sheets)
- ☐ A roll of masking tape
- ☐ A book

Now you and your teammates are ready to build your structure.

1. Use the paper and tape to build a structure at least 12 inches tall that will support the weight of the book. You can build your structure any way you like, but it must be portable. In other words, you are not allowed to fasten it to a table or any other fixed object.

Before you begin building, brainstorm some possible design ideas. All team members should contribute suggestions. Sketch some possible ideas in the space below.

2. After you have built your structure, test it by placing the book on top. Can your structure support the book? Can it support a second book? How much total weight can it hold?

_____

3. Compare your structure with your classmates' creations. Suppose one sheet of paper costs $5 and one inch of tape costs $1. How much did your structure cost?

_____

4. Whose structure holds the most weight for the least amount of money?

_____

ACTIVITY—SCIENCE AND MATHEMATICS

http://antarcticsun.usap.gov/index.cfm

Did you know that Antarctica has its own newspaper? It's true! The *Antarctic Sun* is part of the U. S. Antarctic Program, and is funded by the National Science Foundation. By reading current and back issues of the *Sun*, you can learn a lot about the work scientists are doing there—plus you can learn what it's like to live in a place where temperatures sometimes fall below –100°F. Fears about global warming, the Antarctic ozone hole, and melting Antarctic ice mean that even more scientists will be living and working in Antarctica in the future.

Visit the *Antarctic Sun* Web site to answer the following questions. (If you don't have Internet access, use library resources to learn about the U.S. Antarctic Program and the work scientists are doing in Antarctica.)

1. Browse through some issues of the *Sun* to find a story about the work scientists are doing in Antarctica. Summarize the story in your own words in the space below.

_____

_____

_____

_____

_____

2. Now read a feature story in the *Sun* to find out about life on the ice. What do people do for fun in Antarctica? What makes people want to travel and work there?

_____

_____

_____

_____

3. Based on what you've learned, do you think you would like to live and work in Antarctica? Why or why not?

_____

_____

_____

_____

ACTIVITY—THINKING ABOUT GLOBALIZATION

Globalization is one of the most important trends in today's world. Globalization involves the transfer of goods, information, and ideas among many countries. Economists study global economic issues and their impact on societies.

1. Determine where some of the items in your home or classroom were made. They can include furniture, school supplies, your own clothing, and anything else that has a label indicating its origins. List the countries below.

_____

_____

2. What types of American products do you think are sold in the countries you named in question 1?

_____

_____

3. Have you encountered any other examples of globalization? Maybe you had dinner in an Indian restaurant recently. Maybe you watched a French movie on your Japanese-made DVD player. List some examples below.

_____

_____

4. Do some library/Internet research on the opinions economists and others have about globalization. You will find that while globalization offers many benefits to the world, it also has some potential drawbacks. Summarize your findings in the graphic organizer below.

Benefits of Globalization	Drawbacks to Globalization
1.	1.
2.	2.
3.	3.

5. Overall, do you think globalization has mostly positive or negative consequences? Use a separate sheet of paper to write one or two paragraphs explaining your opinion. Use the information you found for question 4 as evidence for your views.

ACTIVITY—ENGINEERING AND TECHNOLOGY

Aeronautical engineers research, design, develop, and test the performance of aircraft, satellites and space vehicles. Aeronautical engineering offers a wide range of roles, and most engineers specialize in a particular area such as design, manufacture, or maintenance. Constant expansion in air travel means that there are many different types of jobs available in aviation.

In this exercise, you will take on the role of an aeronautical engineer. Your mission is to design and construct three paper airplanes and determine which one travels the greatest distance.

Before you begin, conduct some library/Internet research for tips for making good paper airplanes. Also review the forces that affect flight:

    ☐ Lift   ☐ Thrust
    ☐ Weight   ☐ Drag (air resistance)

Now you are ready to build your airplanes. You will need:

    ☐ Paper for making airplanes   ☐ Ruler or measuring tape

1. Use the paper to make three different airplanes. Try a different design for each. After you are done, use the space below to explain how your planes are different and how they are the same.

_____

_____

_____

2. Before you test your airplanes, predict which one will travel the farthest. Explain your answer.

_____

_____

_____

3. Now fly each airplane three times, using the same amount of force for each flight. Record the distance for each flight in the table below:

	Plane #1	Plane #2	Plane #3
Distance of flight 1			
Distance of flight 2			
Distance of flight 3			

4. What effect do you think heavier paper might have made on your results?

_____

_____

_____

ACTIVITY—SCIENCE AND MATHEMATICS

Like fingerprints, each person's handwriting is unique. When forensic scientists try to identify someone's handwriting, they often examine the way the lines are formed in the letters. People usually slant their writing in a particular way. Some dot their *i's* with circles; some don't dot them at all. Forensic scientists use these and many other clues to help them identify handwriting. In this exercise, you will work with a partner on the following case:

Andrea was absent from school yesterday. Today she gave her teacher, Mr. Chips, a note she said her mother wrote. Mr. Chips suspected that Andrea had actually cut class. Andrea finally admitted that she cut class yesterday and had one of her friends write the excuse note. But she would not tell Mr. Chips who wrote the note, because she didn't want to get anyone else in trouble. Your job is to compare the note Andrea gave Mr. Chips with five other samples to determine who actually wrote the note.

1. First, do some library/Internet research using the keywords *handwriting analysis*. What do forensic scientists look for to detect forgeries? Record your findings on a separate sheet of paper.

2. Both you and your partner need to have five different people write the following on a piece of notebook paper in cursive.

Dear Mr. Chips:
Please excuse Andrea's absence from school yesterday. She had a cold.
Sincerely,
Mrs. Fisher

Ask one of the people to write the same note a second time. The person should try to disguise his/her handwriting in the second note. Select one of this writer's notes to represent the one Andrea gave her teacher.

3. You should have a total of six writing samples. Number them and make a separate list of the numbers. Beside each number, write the name of the person who wrote that note.

4. Keep the note you selected as Andrea's note aside and put the others in an envelope. Your partner should do the same with his/her notes. Exchange all six notes with your partner. Now compare Andrea's note with each of the five samples, looking for similar characteristics. Record your findings in the table below.

	Letter size	Letter slant	Letter spacing	Word spacing	Other characteristics
Andrea's note					
Note 1					
Note 2					
Note 3					
Note 4					
Note 5					

5. Based on your analysis, who do you think wrote the note Andrea gave Mr. Chips?

ACTIVITY—SCIENCE AND MATHEMATICS

Meteorologists study and forecast the weather and climate by interpreting observations of the Earth's surface, oceans, and upper atmosphere. They use satellite photos, computers, and instruments such as barometers to collect data on air pressure and anemometers to collect data on wind speed to make long- and short-term weather forecasts.

People have always been interested in the weather. In the days before meteorologists, people used the world around them to understand and predict the weather. They used the patterns of clouds, the colors of leaves on trees, and the behavior of animals as clues. But did that weather lore have any scientific basis?

Below are several common weather sayings and traditional methods for predicting the weather. Use library/Internet research to determine how accurate these methods are.

1. "Halo around the moon, rain or snow soon."

_____

_____

2. If a wooly caterpillar's red center stripe is wide, winter will be short and mild. If the stripe is narrow, winter will be long and harsh.

_____

_____

3. "Red sky at night, sailor's delight. Red sky in the morning, sailor's warning."

_____

_____

4. It is possible to use cricket chirps to gauge the current temperature.

_____

_____

5. In the space below, record a weather saying you've heard a friend or family member make. Then do some research to find out how scientifically accurate it is.

_____

_____

_____

ACTIVITY—IT'S A-MAZE-ING!

Do you like to work puzzles? Have you ever made one of your own? A **maze** is a type of puzzle with a series of paths. To solve the puzzle, you have to find your way through the maze to the end. It takes great skill to design a good maze. Here's a simple example:

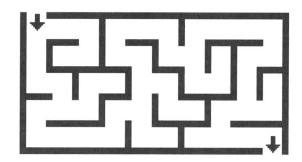

Use a separate sheet of plain or graph paper to create your own maze. Here are a few tips that will help you make a great maze:

1. Start your drawing with a pencil; this will make it easier to erase mistakes.

2. Use a ruler to draw a large square or rectangle. A 4" x 4" square would be a good size and shape to start with.

3. Using the ruler to measure, lightly draw a dot every half centimeter along each side. Then connect the dots with straight lines. You should now have a grid of 100 boxes.

4. Pick a starting and ending point. Sketch a route through the grid from the start point to the end point. Work in plenty of twists and turns to make your finished maze more difficult. Be sure to make a few turns that look like they are going to lead somewhere but only end up as dead-ends. This will really confuse anyone who tries to solve your puzzle!

5. When you are finished, use a pen to trace over the walls of your maze. Be careful not to put any walls across the actual path to the ending point. And don't forget to indicate the Start and Finish of your puzzle at the right locations.

6. Finally, erase any visible pencil marks. Now your maze is ready! Be sure to make copies of the original before giving the puzzle to your friends to solve.

You can find more tips for drawing mazes in the library or online at Web sites such as http://www.amazeingart.com. Have fun!

EXPLORING A CAREER IN THE SCIENCE, TECHNOLOGY, ENGINEERING & MATHEMATICS CLUSTER

The O*NET program (http://online.onetcenter.org/) is the nation's primary source of occupational information. O*NET provides data on thousands of specific jobs, including typical tasks, knowledge/skills, work styles, and education required by each. Visit the O*NET site to complete this activity. (If you do not have Internet access, gather information from your library's print version of the *Occupational Outlook Handbook*.)

1. Click the Find Occupations link. In the Quick Search box, enter a job title from the Science, Technology, Engineering & Mathematics Career Cluster that interests you. View the Details report.

(*Note:* Sample occupations in this Career Cluster can be found at the www.careerclusters.org Web site or from your teacher.)

2. Use the information you find at O*NET to fill out the following chart for the job title you chose. List the top three characteristics of the items with an asterisk (*).

Tasks*	Tools & Technology*	Knowledge*	Skills*
Abilities*	Work Activities*	Work Context*	Interests*
Work Styles*	Work Values*	Work Needs*	Related Occupations
Education Required	Median Wages	Employment	Projected Growth

3. Would you be interested in this job? Why or why not?

_____

_____

_____

Passions
☐ Being creative and original
☐ Using music, art, drama, or writing
☐ Applying technology

Attitude
☐ Persistent
☐ Creative and unique

Talents
☐ Innovative style
☐ Technical and mechanical ability
☐ Art, music, drama, or writing ability

Heart
☐ Likes to create original ideas or objects
☐ Needs variety in activities

Some Career Areas to Consider
☐ Graphic designer
☐ Journalist
☐ Lighting technician
☐ Scriptwriter
☐ Interior designer

Employment Outlook
☐ Employment within AV industries is expected to grow by 21 to 35 percent for the foreseeable future.
☐ Nearly 7 out of 10 visual artists are self-employed.
☐ Jobs in telecommunications and journalism are expected to experience slow growth, while graphic artists will be in demand.

ACTIVITY—AUDIO AND VIDEO TECHNOLOGY AND FILM

Recording good music requires more than just talented musicians. A typical recording studio is divided into two rooms—a performance space and a control room—separated by a window. The performance space is designed to block outside noise. This is where the musicians perform. The control room contains the recording equipment and **mixing console**, or **sound board**. The mixing console is the main control device. All the recording equipment is connected to it.

In the control room a producer, audio engineer, and technicians work together. The producer makes the artistic decisions about the kind of sound music-buyers want. The audio engineer oversees the technical side of the recording session. The engineer and technicians position the microphones and operate the recording equipment.

The sound of each voice and instrument is captured with a different microphone. Each signal is fed into the mixing console. The audio engineer uses the console to adjust the sound qualities of each instrument and voice separately. The engineer then routes the sounds to a multitrack recorder. **Tracks** are narrow strips that run the length of the surface of the audiotape. Each sound input is recorded on its own track.

Often parts of a song are recorded at different times. The guitars and drums might be recorded first and the voices of the singers later. The singers wear headphones to hear the already-recorded background music as they sing. Through a process called overdubbing, the audio engineer can layer new musical parts onto already-recorded parts. Overdubbing makes it possible, for example, for a guitarist to play both the lead and base guitar parts, or for a singer to harmonize with herself.

Once all the musical parts have been assembled on tracks, the sounds are played back through the mixing console. The audio engineer works with the producer to select the pieces to include in the final version. The engineer uses the console's controls to shape the final sounds. The engineer can erase mistakes, take out unwanted parts, and adjust the sound qualities, such as loudness and tone, of each track. The engineer can even rearrange parts, if desired.

When editing is complete, the engineer combines the parts into the required number of tracks. Stereo sound requires two tracks. Surround-sound requires six tracks. The recording process concludes with a **master**, from which the music is duplicated for distribution to the public.

Directions: Use the information from the article and your own experiences to answer the following questions.

1. **Describing** How is a recording studio arranged?

_____

_____

_____

_____

_____

2. **Problem-Solving** Suppose the drummer did not show up for the recording session. How might the audio engineer handle this situation?

_____

_____

_____

_____

_____

3. **Analyzing** Suppose a band has one singer. The band's hit song was created in the studio by overdubbing the singer's voice doing multiple parts in harmony. How might this affect the way the band performs the song live?

_____

_____

_____

_____

_____

4. **Describing** What are some ways that the audio engineer can shape the sounds in a recording during the mixing process?

_____

_____

_____

_____

_____

5. **Assessing** What kinds of personal characteristics does a music producer need? Which of these characteristics do _you_ have?

_____

_____

_____

_____

_____

6. **Assessing** What kinds of personal characteristics does an audio engineer need? Which of these characteristics do _you_ have?

_____

_____

_____

_____

_____

ORGANIZING CAREER CHOICES

Directions: Choose one of the following occupations from the Arts, A/V Technology & Communications Cluster: set designer, cartoonist, commercial photographer, or playwright. Then use the following table to compare and contrast it with an occupation from another Career Cluster of your choice. Finally, tell which job would suit you best. Conduct library/Internet research to locate the necessary information.

Hint: The *Occupational Outlook Handbook* (OOH) is available in most public libraries and is a good source of career information. Your school counselor's office may also have career information available. The online version of the OOH [http://www.bls.gov/oco/] is a good starting point for Internet research.

	Arts, A/V Technology & Communications occupation:	Other occupation:
Qualifications/training		
Earnings		
Employment outlook		
Working conditions		
Typical duties		
Similar occupations		
Additional sources of information about this occupation		

Which of these two jobs would suit you better? Why?

_____

_____

ACTIVITY—VISUAL ARTS

You have probably enjoyed watching cartoon movies. Have you ever wondered how animators make their characters move? In the early days of cartoon films, animators made a series of drawings on paper. In each drawing, the characters changed position slightly from one to the next. The filmmaker photographed the series, with each drawing becoming one frame of film. When the film was played through a projector, the characters appeared to move. Today, animators combine hand-drawings with computer technology to create the illusion of movement. By creating your own "flick book," you can get an idea of how still drawings can come to life.

Materials you will need:

☐   5 sheets of paper, cut into fourths,
      either on a pad or stapled together at one edge
☐   a pencil

Steps:

1. Choose a simple movement you want your character to perform. You could have him walk, turn a cartwheel, or dance, for example.

2. Visualize the character making this movement in slow motion. Notice how the limbs move.

3. Draw a simple stick figure on the last page of the pad.

4. On the previous page, trace the stick figure, only this time change the positions of his arms and legs just a little. The change should be in the direction you visualized for the character's movement.

5. Continue tracing the previous drawing, each time changing the position of the arms and legs slightly as the movement progresses.

6. When you use up all the pages, flick the book from back to front to see your character move.

Do you think you would like to work as an animator? Why or why not?

_____

_____

_____

_____

_____

ACTIVITY—TELECOMMUNICATIONS

Telecommunications refers to the transmission of signals over distances for the purpose of communicating. For example, telecommunications signals are transmitted by cell phones, televisions, radios, and computers. The process requires sophisticated equipment—and telecommunications technicians to install, operate, and repair it.

Do library or online research to learn how cell phones work. Use what you learn to answer the following questions.

1. What does a cell phone transmit?

_____

2. In a cell phone system, what is a cell?

_____

_____

3. What is the purpose of a cell tower?

_____

_____

4. You have been traveling in a car for quite some distance, yet you have continued your cell phone conversation without interruption. How is this possible?

_____

_____

_____

5. You are hiking in the wilderness. You decide to call a friend to tell her about your adventure. You pull out your cell phone and . . . it doesn't work. Why not?

_____

_____

_____

6. You are on an airplane sitting on a runway. To kill some time, you pull out your cell phone. But before you can dial, a recorded message says, "Turn off all cell phones and other electronic devices." Why is this necessary?

_____

_____

_____

ACTIVITY—JOURNALISM AND BROADCASTING

In this activity, you will work in groups of three to prepare and present a three-minute television news story. Follow these steps:

☐   With your partners, discuss events in your school or community that might be newsworthy. Select one as the focus for your group's work.

☐   Watch television news broadcasts on a station such as CNN or Fox News. Take notes about the kinds of facts included in a news story and how the story is presented.

1. What does a news anchor do?

_____

_____

2. What does a reporter do?

_____

_____

3. What does a news analyst do?

_____

_____

☐   Research the story you selected.

☐   Together with your group, select the facts you want to present.

☐   Collaborate with your group to write a script to present the story. Your script should include the roles of news anchor, reporter, and news analyst.

☐   Decide which group member will perform each role.

☐   Practice presenting your story in the style of a television news broadcast.

☐   Present your story to the class.

4. Based on this activity, do you think you would enjoy a career in broadcast journalism? Why or why not?

_____

_____

_____

_____

_____

ACTIVITY—PERFORMING ARTS

Do you have a flair for drama? Does performing in front of a group energize you? Then maybe you would enjoy an acting career. Acting may look easy. After, it's just talking and moving— things you do all the time, right? Try this activity . . . It may be more challenging than you think!

- ☐ Record an episode from a television show or rent a movie you like from a video store.
- ☐ Choose a scene in which an actor is speaking and making fairly simple movements.
- ☐ Practice saying the lines with the actor. Try to imitate the actor's tone of voice, timing, and lip movements as you memorize the lines.
- ☐ Then try to imitate the actor's gestures, facial expressions, and movements on stage as you play the scene.
- ☐ Continue playing the scene over and over until you feel comfortable with the speech and movements.
- ☐ Now turn off the sound and lip-sync the lines and move as the actor moves.
- ☐ Perform the scene in front of a mirror, without the recording.
- ☐ Finally, perform the scene for a small group of friends or family.

1. Evaluate your own performance. What did you do well? What could you improve?

_____

_____

_____

_____

2. What parts of the exercise were easiest for you? voice tone? gestures? movement? something else? What parts were more difficult?

_____

_____

_____

3. How did performing for a group make you feel? Were you scared? excited? energized? self-conscious? intimidated? Based on this experience, do you think you have what it takes to be an actor? Why or why not?

_____

_____

_____

_____

ACTIVITY—PRINTING TECHNOLOGY

Desktop publishing is the use of computers and special software to create documents such as newsletters, pamphlets, flyers, and even books. Using desktop publishing software, you can combine graphics with text in an attractive layout. You can then print the final electronic file on your own printer, or have it printed commercially.

In this activity, you will use desktop publishing software to create a common document: a business card. If you do not have access to software, create the business card manually by placing sketches or cut-out graphics with text on a cardboard backing. Your card will be 3.5" wide by 2" high.

Business people exchange business cards when they meet. Your business card should give basic information about you to help the other person remember you. A typical card includes:

- Your name and job title
- Name of your business
- Street address
- Phone number(s)

- Email address
- Web site address
- Brief phrase describing your business
- Logo or other graphic element

Although business cards are a recent invention, you will create a business card for a famous person in history. For example, Benjamin Franklin was a printer and inventor. Imagine the text and graphic he might have used to create a memorable business card.

Choose a historical figure for your card, and follow these steps:

1. Bring in a business card from an adult and combine it with those collected by other students. Examine the class's card collection to see how business cards are designed.

2. Read about the historical person you selected to learn more about the person's business affiliation and accomplishments. Choose a memorable accomplishment to feature on the card.

3. Write a phrase that captures this accomplishment. You don't have much room, so keep it brief. Use abbreviations, if needed. Make up the street addresses, phone numbers, and online addresses. For example, Ben Franklin's email address might be bfranklin@kite.com.

4. Create a graphic element using clip art or a downloaded graphic, or sketch one.

5. Plan the card layout by doing rough sketches of different locations for the text and graphic.

6. Choose a template in your software, or create your own design.

7. Combine the text and graphic into a finished business card.

Do you think you would like a job as a desktop publishing specialist? Why or why not?

_____

_____

_____

EXPLORING A CAREER IN THE ARTS, A/V TECHNOLOGY & COMMUNICATIONS CLUSTER

The O*NET program (http://online.onetcenter.org/) is the nation's primary source of occupational information. O*NET provides data on thousands of specific jobs, including typical tasks, knowledge/skills, work styles, and education required by each. Visit the O*NET site to complete this activity. (If you do not have Internet access, gather information from your library's print version of the *Occupational Outlook Handbook*.)

1. Click the Find Occupations link. In the Quick Search box, enter a job title from the Arts, A/V Technology & Communications Career Cluster that interests you. View the Details report.

(*Note:* Sample occupations in this Career Cluster can be found at the www.careerclusters.org Web site or from your teacher.)

2. Use the information you find at O*NET to fill out the following chart for the job title you chose. List the top three characteristics of the items with an asterisk (*).

Tasks*	Tools & Technology*	Knowledge*	Skills*
Abilities*	Work Activities*	Work Context*	Interests*
Work Styles*	Work Values*	Work Needs*	Related Occupations
Education Required	Median Wages	Employment	Projected Growth

3. Would you be interested in this job? Why or why not?

_____

_____

_____

Passions
- ☐ Solving problems
- ☐ Trying new technology
- ☐ Improving how things work

Attitude
- ☐ Analytical
- ☐ Curious

Talents
- ☐ Ability to work with technology
- ☐ Scientific-minded
- ☐ Detail-oriented

Heart
- ☐ Likes to work alone
- ☐ Likes challenge of solving problems

Some Career Areas to Consider
- ☐ Multimedia producer
- ☐ Network administrator
- ☐ Game programmer
- ☐ Database administrator
- ☐ Graphic artist

Employment Outlook
- ☐ People with IT skills are needed in organizations of all sizes.
- ☐ Job growth is expected to be faster than average in almost all areas of this Career Cluster. Opportunities will likely be greatest for software engineers and workers in the interactive media and information support and services pathways.

ACTIVITY—INFORMATION SUPPORT AND SERVICES

A **technical writer** uses simple language to explain difficult scientific and technical ideas to average readers. Many technical writers produce instruction manuals that go with products. Others prepare **documentation**, which is any material used to explain something about a system or procedure. Common types of information technology (IT) documentation include user guides, online help guides, and FAQs (Frequently Asked Questions). Technical writers also work frequently with engineers and designers to prepare written interpretations of engineering and design specifications and other information for a general audience

IT businesses employ thousands of technical writers. In addition, technical writers often work as self-employed "freelance" writers who sell their work to publishers or other businesses. They are paid by the job or by the hour. Sometimes they are hired to do specific jobs such as writing about a new high-tech product.

For more than 20 years, Kate McCall has been writing documentation and product manuals for a variety of IT businesses. On the next page she gives us an idea of what her work is like.

Kate, what kind of experience do you need to get into technical writing?

I have a bachelor's degree and a master's degree in Computer Science. I worked as a computer programmer for a time before turning to technical writing. I think it helps for technical writers to have at least some technical background. However, I work with many very good technical writers who have degrees in English, journalism, and other nontechnical areas.

Is it difficult to become a technical writer?

In a way. There's a great demand for technical writers, but the main obstacle is experience. Job applicants tend to either understand the technical details but aren't good at communicating them, or they're good writers but they don't "get" the science.

What do you like most about your job?

I take a lot of satisfaction in pulling together complicated information and making it easy to understand. Not only do I get to help someone use the product, I get to learn about how different products and processes work.

Besides excellent writing skills, what do you need to be a good technical writer?

*People skills. I work with a lot of engineers, so I really need to be willing to seek information and take advice from them in order to get a manual written. Technical training helps too—HTML, Web design, knowledge of different kinds of software. And you **really** need to be tuned in to who is going to be reading what you're writing—their education level and familiarity with the product. More than anything, that drives how the manual will be written.*

Directions: Use the information from the article and your own experiences to answer the following questions.

1. **Defining** What is a technical writer?

_____

_____

_____

2. **Differentiating** How is a freelance technical writer different from a technical writer employed by an IT company?

_____

_____

_____

_____

3. **Critical Thinking** Name two companies that would be likely to hire a technical writer. What duties would the technical writer perform at these companies?

_____

_____

_____

_____

4. **Hypothesizing** Why do you think a software company needs a technical writer to prepare instruction manuals? Why might a technical writer be a better choice for this job than the computer programmer who actually created the software?

_____

_____

_____

_____

5. **Making Connections** Have you ever tried to assemble or use a product with poorly written instructions? How did this make you feel? Were you able to use the product successfully even with the inadequate instructions?

_____

_____

_____

_____

6. **Assessing** Based on the article, what kinds of personal characteristics does a good technical writer need? How many of these characteristics do _you_ have?

_____

_____

_____

_____

ORGANIZING CAREER CHOICES

Directions: Choose one of the following occupations from the Information Technology Cluster: PC support specialist, application integrator, operating systems designer, or webmaster. Then use the following table to compare and contrast it with an occupation from another Career Cluster of your choice. Finally, tell which job would suit you best. Conduct library/Internet research to locate the necessary information.

Hint: The *Occupational Outlook Handbook* (OOH) is available in most public libraries and is a good source of career information. Your school counselor's office may also have career information available. The online version of the OOH [http://www.bls.gov/oco/] is a good starting point for Internet research.

	Information Technology occupation:	**Other occupation:**
Qualifications/training		
Earnings		
Employment outlook		
Working conditions		
Typical duties		
Similar occupations		
Additional sources of information about this occupation		

Which of these two jobs would suit you better? Why?

_____

_____

ACTIVITY—PROGRAMMING AND SOFTWARE DEVELOPMENT

Software developers are often asked to solve a puzzle as part of a job interview. Often these puzzles have no single right answer. Sometimes they don't have a right answer at all! They're designed to test how logically (and quickly) a job candidate can think. Try your hand at some classic puzzles that have been challenging developers for years. Write your answers on a separate sheet of paper. (Your teacher has some possible solutions for each problem.)

The Rope Bridge

Four explorers must cross a wobbly rope bridge to get back to their camp for the night. But they have only one flashlight, and the batteries are low. In 17 minutes the flashlight will no longer work. The bridge is too dangerous to cross in the dark, and it can support only two people at any given time.

Each explorer walks at a different speed. One can cross the bridge in 1 minute, another in 2 minutes, the third in 5 minutes, and the fourth in 10 minutes. How do the explorers make it across in 17 minutes?

ABCDE Puzzle

In the sequence puzzle at the right, what comes in the five cells shown with a question mark?

A	B	C	D	E
C	A	D	BC	E
	CD	A		EC
DB		C	A	DE
?	?	?	?	?

The Card Game

I offer to play a card game with you using a normal deck of 52 cards. We will turn over two cards at a time. If the cards are both black, they go into my pile. If they are both red, they go into your pile. If there is one red and one black, they go into the discard pile.

We play the game until we've gone through all 52 cards, then we each count the number of cards we have. If there is a tie, I win. Otherwise, you win. The loser pays the winner a dollar. How much would you pay to play this game?

Item	Value	Weight
Box A	$40	12 pounds
Box B	$20	1 pound
Box C	$100	4 pounds
Box D	$10	1 pound
Box E	$20	2 pounds

The Knapsack Problem

Given the information in the table at left, which boxes should be chosen to put inside a knapsack in order to (a) pack the most money while (b) still keeping the overall weight under 15 pounds?

ACTIVITY—GARBAGE IN-GARBAGE OUT

There is a famous rule in information technology: **garbage in-garbage out**. This means that if a computer programmer provides inaccurate or incorrect steps (garbage), the computer will output garbage as well. Or, if a software manual omits a step in the installation procedure, the user will not be able to use the software properly. It is very important to be precise when providing directions in the world of information technology.

In this activity, you are going to work with a partner. (a) Each of you will write detailed instructions about how to lace and tie a gym shoe. (b) You and your partner will test the precision of each other's instructions. Before you begin, each of you will need an unlaced gym shoe and the shoelace that goes in it.

1. Now, in the space below, write very detailed step-by-step instructions about how to lace and tie a gym shoe. Assume that the lace is completely out of the shoe at the beginning.

_____

_____

_____

_____

_____

_____

_____

_____

_____

_____

_____

2. After you and your partner are finished writing, exchange instructions and read them. Then each of you should take one of the shoes and follow the other partner's instructions *exactly*. You will discover where the instructions are clear and where they are not.

Does the "program" your partner has written result in the desired outcome: a laced and tied gym shoe? Explain.

_____

_____

_____

ACTIVITY—INTERACTIVE MEDIA

A **home page** is the first page seen by a visitor to a Web site. In this activity, you are going to sketch a home page for your very own Web site. Your site can be about you, about a favorite pastime (sports team, band, hobby), or about a local attraction you enjoy.

You can learn about good Web site design by visiting and studying some award-winning Web sites. Find some examples by visiting www.worldbestwebsites.com or search online using the keywords *best designed Web sites*. You will also need to do some library/Internet research about basic Web design principles. Use the *Readers' Guide to Periodical Literature* or search online using the keywords *web design tips*.

1. Use the following table to generate a list of design elements you will—and will not—want to use for your home page.

Design elements I will use	Design elements I will avoid
Text that is large enough to read, but not too big Lots of white space	Paragraphs written in all caps or all bold Background images

2. In the space below, state the subject and write two or three goals for your home page.

_____

_____

_____

(continued on next page)

3. Now think about the people you want to visit your site. What elements and information can you include on your home page that will interest them?

For example, will your home page include text only, or will you use other media elements such as graphics (pictures), animation, or sound? Will you provide hyperlinks to other Web sites that might interest your audience? (A **hyperlink** is a graphic or line of text on a Web page that takes you to another place on the Internet.) Record them in the table below.

Media elements I will use	Hyperlinks I will use

4. Finally, use the space below to sketch out your home page.

ACTIVITY—THE HISTORY OF THE INTERNET

http://www.computerhistory.org/

The history of the development of the Internet is a fascinating and important story. Many Web sites document the technical milestones of Internet development. It is interesting to note how quickly the Internet has grown into its current form. Go to the computerhistory.org Web site and click the Internet History link, or use other online or library resources (keywords *Internet history* or *Internet timeline*) to answer the following questions.

1. Using information you find in your research, draw a simple Internet timeline in the space below. Note the most important milestones in the development of the Internet.

2. What do you consider the most important Internet development to take place in the 1980s? Why?

_____

_____

_____

3. Do you use the Internet regularly? What for? (If you do not use the 'Net regularly, tell why not. Name one way it might help you in your schoolwork.)

_____

_____

_____

4. Do you think the Internet could be improved? How? For example, could it be made more secure or easier to use? Do you think you have the skills to help make that improvement? Why or why not?

_____

_____

_____

_____

ACTIVITY—NETWORK SYSTEMS

Malware is short for *malicious software*, a computer program or file designed to damage or disrupt a system. Examples of malware include viruses, worms, and Trojan horses. A **virus** is a program or piece of code that is loaded onto your computer without your knowledge and runs against your wishes. A **Trojan horse** is a destructive program that pretends to be a safe program; they differ from viruses because they do not replicate (reproduce) themselves inside your computer. A **worm** is a program that replicates itself over a computer network and usually performs malicious actions.

Network administrators must safeguard their companies' computer systems against malware. In this activity, you are going to use library/Internet resources to compile a list of guidelines employees should follow to protect their computers from malware. Two tips have been provided to get you started. Fill the page with others.

☐ Install an anti-virus program and update it regularly.
☐ Do not open an e-mail attachment from someone you do not know.

_____

_____

_____

_____

_____

_____

_____

_____

_____

_____

_____

_____

_____

_____

ACTIVITY—PROGRAMMING AND SOFTWARE DEVELOPMENT

What is the best software program of all time? What is the worst? IT professionals have very strong opinions on this topic. If you are a regular computer user, you probably do too. Microsoft Windows ME and Microsoft Bob frequently make the "all-time worst" lists. So does the IBM/OS2. "All-time best" software choices include Netscape Navigator, Aldus PageMaker, and WordPerfect 5.1.

Do some library/Internet research on the best (and worst) software programs ever. Use keywords like *best software* and *worst software* to help you. (The August 14, 2006 issue of *Information Week* has an article entitled, "What's the Greatest Software Ever Written?" by Charles Babcock. The article is available in print or online and would be a good starting point.)

Now answer some questions about the great and not-so-great software products you have used.

1. Describe the best software program you have ever used. Why did you like it so much?

_____

_____

_____

2. Describe the worst software program you have ever used. Why did you dislike it so much?

_____

_____

_____

3. Have you ever had an idea for a new software program? Can you think of a way one of your favorite programs or games could be even better? Could it use an extra feature or graphic? Write your ideas on a separate page.

_____

_____

_____

_____

_____

_____

_____

EXPLORING A CAREER IN THE INFORMATION TECHNOLOGY CLUSTER

The O*NET program (http://online.onetcenter.org/) is the nation's primary source of occupational information. O*NET provides data on thousands of specific jobs, including typical tasks, knowledge/skills, work styles, and education required by each. Visit the O*NET site to complete this activity. (If you do not have Internet access, gather information from your library's print version of the *Occupational Outlook Handbook*.)

1. Click the Find Occupations link. In the Quick Search box, enter a job title from the Information Technology Career Cluster that interests you. View the Details report.

(*Note:* Sample occupations in this Career Cluster can be found at the www.careerclusters.org Web site or from your teacher.)

2. Use the information you find at O*NET to fill out the following chart for the job title you chose. List the top three characteristics of the items with an asterisk (*).

Tasks*	Tools & Technology*	Knowledge*	Skills*
Abilities*	Work Activities*	Work Context*	Interests*
Work Styles*	Work Values*	Work Needs*	Related Occupations
Education Required	Median Wages	Employment	Projected Growth

3. Would you be interested in this job? Why or why not?

_____

_____

_____

Name _____

Date _____

Passions
- ☐ Planning and organizing
- ☐ Working with hands or using technology
- ☐ Working outdoors and/or with animals

Attitude
- ☐ High energy
- ☐ Common sense

Talents
- ☐ Technical skills
- ☐ Problem-solving ability
- ☐ Math and science ability

Heart
- ☐ Likes to work independently
- ☐ Likes to learn how systems work

Some Career Areas to Consider
- ☐ Park ranger
- ☐ Meteorologist
- ☐ Veterinarian
- ☐ Botanist
- ☐ Recycling technician

Employment Outlook
- ☐ Continued globalization will spur growth in food and natural resources, especially for those who understand international markets.
- ☐ Growing world population will increase the demand for scientists and technologists in food and fiber.
- ☐ Rising public health concerns will increase demand for jobs in environmental services.

ACTIVITY—FOOD PRODUCTS AND PROCESSING SYSTEMS

Traditional farm methods rely on chemical fertilizers and pesticides to produce crops. However, overuse or improper use of these chemicals can pollute the environment. Chemicals from farm runoff (water that drains or flows off of the land surface) can seep into the ground water, contaminating local water supplies. Pesticides sprayed on crops can travel in the wind to nearby streams. Fertilizers and pesticides can also interfere with the soil's natural system for breaking down wastes and releasing nutrients. As a result, the soil can become less productive.

Concerns for the health of the environment and of the foods we eat have spurred the growth of organic farming. **Organic farming** is a system of agriculture that relies on natural substances rather than on synthetic chemicals for raising crops and livestock. Organic farmers use *manure* (animal wastes) or *compost* (decaying organic matter) as fertilizers. To replace the nutrients in the soil, organic farmers rotate their crops. They might grow corn in a field one year and soybeans in that field the next year. Corn uses nitrogen from the soil. The roots of legumes, like soybeans, hold beneficial bacteria that can replace the nitrogen in the soil.

Crop rotation also helps control insect pests and plant diseases. Insects and diseases typically affect only certain plants. Those attracted to corn will die out when corn is replaced by soybeans in that field. Organic farmers might also enlist the help of the pests' natural enemies, such as ladybugs and other beneficial insects that prey on insect pests.

Organic farming extends to livestock as well. Organically raised animals eat only 100 percent organic feed. They do not receive growth hormones or antibiotics. These animals also have access to the outdoors. In non-organic "factory farms," animals are raised in buildings to make them easier to manage. Feeding and watering are controlled mechanically. In organic farming, however, animals are allowed to graze in outdoor pastures.

The U.S. Department of Agriculture (USDA) has set standards for organic foods. Before a food can be labeled "organic," USDA-approved certifiers inspect the farms and the companies that process the foods to make sure they are following all the rules set for organic foods. Here are the standards set by the USDA for food labeling:

☐ **"100% Organic":** All ingredients must be organic. These foods are allowed to carry the USDA Organic seal.
☐ **"Organic":** At least 95 percent of the ingredients must be organic. These foods are also allowed to carry the USDA Organic seal.
☐ **"Made with Organic Ingredients":** At least 70 percent of the ingredients must be organic. These foods cannot carry the USDA Organic seal.
☐ **"Free-range," "Hormone-free,"** or **"Natural":** These claims are truthful, but should not be confused with organic foods.

As a consumer of organic foods, you benefit from eating foods free of toxic pesticides. Organic farming also reduces the flow of harmful chemicals into the soil and water supplies. Organic farming is often called "sustainable farming" because it helps preserve healthy ecosystems and the productivity of the soil for future generations.

> *"Organic Agriculture should sustain and enhance the health of soil, plant, animal, human and planet as one and indivisible."*
> —International Federation of Organic Agriculture Movements (IFOAM)

Directions: Use the information from the article and your own experiences to answer the following questions.

1. **Contrasting** How do organic methods differ from traditional farming methods?

_____

_____

_____

_____

2. **Identifying** What are the benefits of crop rotation?

_____

_____

_____

_____

_____

3. **Explaining** Why might a food processor want to label its product "Organic"?

_____

_____

_____

_____

_____

4. **Analyzing** If a food label says "All Natural," is it organic? How do you know?

_____

_____

_____

_____

_____

5. **Drawing Conclusions** How do you benefit from organic farming?

_____

_____

_____

_____

6. **Assessing** Based on the article, what kinds of personal characteristics does a good organic farmer need? Which of these characteristics do _you_ have?

_____

_____

_____

_____

ORGANIZING CAREER CHOICES

Directions: Choose one of the following occupations from the Agriculture, Food & Natural Resources Cluster: tree surgeon, wildlife manager, water quality manager, or ranch manager. Then use the following table to compare and contrast it with an occupation from another Career Cluster of your choice. Finally, tell which job would suit you best. Conduct library/Internet research to locate the necessary information.

Hint: The *Occupational Outlook Handbook* (OOH) is available in most public libraries and is a good source of career information. Your school counselor's office may also have career information available. The online version of the OOH [http://www.bls.gov/oco/] is a good starting point for Internet research.

	Agriculture, Food & Natural Resources occupation:	**Other occupation:**
Qualifications/training		
Earnings		
Employment outlook		
Working conditions		
Typical duties		
Similar occupations		
Additional sources of information about this occupation		

Which of these two jobs would suit you better? Why?

_____

_____

ACTIVITY—PLANT SYSTEMS

Live plants enhance the beauty of the landscape around homes and offices. People often hire landscape designers to choose the plants and design the arrangement. Good landscape designers know the plants that grow well in the area. They also know the characteristics of each plant. For example, some plants have a narrow growth pattern and will fit a tight space. Others need room because they grow tall and full. Landscape designers also understand the conditions in which each plant grows best. A plant that requires full sunlight to thrive would not do well planted beneath shade trees. Each plant has special characteristics that make it attractive. Some have colorful blossoms. Others turn color or produce berries in the fall or have interesting leaf shapes.

Visit a garden store or greenhouse that carries plants for home landscaping. Pick out six plants that interest you. Read the informational tags to help you complete the chart below. If the tags do not contain all the information you need, ask a store employee.

Plant Name	Sun or Shade?	Growth Pattern	Special Features

Select a place in your yard that would benefit from some landscaping. Measure the area. Draw a landscape design on graph paper, roughly to scale. Choose two or three plants from the chart. Show the location of each plant and label each by name. Be sure to consider how large each plant grows. Low-growing plants next to the house could be hidden by tall, bushy shrubs in front of them.

On a separate page, tell if you think you would enjoy working as a landscape designer. Why or why not?

ACTIVITY—NATURAL RESOURCE SYSTEMS

Whether you manage a wildlife sanctuary, forest, or coastal fishery, an important part of your job is to help preserve a healthy ecosystem. An **ecosystem** is made up of all living things in the area as well as their physical environment, including air, water, and soil. Organisms depend on one another and their environment to live. To see how this works, create a food web.

Step 1. Use your word processor to create separate text boxes containing the following information. Place the text boxes spaced out on a document page. If you do not have access to a computer, write the information within drawn boxes, spaced out on a sheet of white paper.

Sun provides energy	**Snakes** eat songbirds and mice	**Songbirds** eat earthworms and insects	**Mice** eat green plants and insects
Green Plants make own food using the sun's energy	**Earthworms** eat dead plants, insects, and animals	**Hawks** eat songbirds, snakes, and mice	**Insects** eat green plants and other insects

Step 2. Begin with the sun. What living thing uses the sun for nourishment? Green plants! Draw an arrow from the sun box to the green-plant box.

Step 3. What depends on green plants for food? Draw arrows from the green-plant box to the living things that feed on them.

Step 4. Continue drawing arrows in this manner until you have included all boxes in the web. Then answer the following questions.

1. If a pesticide killed the insects in this ecosystem, how would other living things be affected?

_____

_____

_____

_____

2. If you were the manager of a wildlife sanctuary, forest, or fishery, why should you be concerned with the health of the entire ecosystem?

_____

_____

_____

_____

ACTIVITY—ENVIRONMENTAL SERVICE SYSTEMS

Clean, fresh water is a critical natural resource. Fresh water supports much of the life on Earth. Yet about 97.5 percent of all the world's water is salt water, leaving 2.5 percent fresh water. Nearly 70 percent of this fresh water is frozen in the polar ice caps. Most of the rest exists as soil moisture. In all, less than 1 percent of Earth's fresh water is available for direct use. We must conserve this precious resource.

1. How much water do you use in an average day? Find an online water use calculator (keywords *water use calculator*) to make an estimate. (You could also figure daily water consumption from your family's most recent water bill.)

What was your total? _____

2. In the chart below, list ten activities that use water in your family's daily life. To the right of each activity, list a way that you and your family could reduce the amount of water you use for that activity.

Water-Use Activity	Ways to Conserve Water

ACTIVITY—PLANT AND ANIMAL SYSTEMS

Researchers in plant and animal systems look for ways to help farmers increase their yields and improve the quality of the foods. Traditionally, researchers have used genetic principles in breeding to produce, for example, bigger cows or corn with fuller ears. In the 1970s, geneticists developed new techniques that became known as genetic engineering.

Genetic engineering is the process of altering the genetic makeup of an organism. It is done by taking DNA from one organism and inserting it into the cells of another organism. Using genetic engineering, researchers can give a farm animal or plant favorable traits. For example, plant geneticists produced a cotton plant that can withstand herbicides. Farmers can then use herbicides to kill weeds without harming the cotton. Animal geneticists used genetically engineered bacteria to produce a growth hormone. Cows given this hormone produce more milk. Some experiments have involved transferring genes between species. For example, researchers tried unsuccessfully to produce a frost-resistant tomato using genes from a fish.

Genetic engineering has produced many benefits for a hungry world. It has also sparked controversy, however. Do some library or online research to learn more about the debate over genetic engineering. Then answer the following questions.

1. What are some benefits of genetic engineering in agriculture?

_____

_____

_____

2. What are some safety concerns about genetic engineering in agriculture?

_____

_____

_____

3. What moral issues are part of this debate?

_____

_____

_____

4. Where do you stand on this issue? Why?

_____

_____

_____

_____

ACTIVITY—YOUR FARM IQ

Extension agents have knowledge in a wide range of farm-related topics. They advise farmers, demonstrate the latest agricultural techniques, and give classes on topics such as feeding and maintaining the health of livestock. Do you have what it takes to be an extension agent? Test your Farm IQ by taking this quiz. Circle the correct answer. Use library or online resources to find answers, if needed. (Your teacher has the answers to this quiz.)

1. What do the four H's in the 4H club stand for?
A Home, Hearth, Health, Hands
B Head, Hands, Heart, Health
C Home, Hearth, Heart, Hands
D Head, Hands, Heart, and Hearth

2. What type of chickens lay brown eggs?
A organic chickens
B old chickens
C free-range chickens
D chickens with red ear lobes

3. Which of these is not a vegetable?
A pumpkin
B turnip
C broccoli
D carrot

4. What is the name for the offspring of a male horse and a female donkey?
A mule
B donkey
C hinny
D stallion

4. What is hominy made from?
A corn
B rice
C potatoes
D squash

5. How many chambers are in a cow's stomach?
A 1
B 2
C 3
D 4

6. What is the name for the process of shining a light through a chicken egg to check for cracks?
A illuminating
B candling
C irradiating
D beaming

7. What does a combine do?
A It is used to mow the grass.
B It is used to milk the cows.
C It separates the stalk from the grain.
D It is the workhorse on the farm.

8. On average, how many ears of corn are on a stalk?
A 1 - 2
B 3 - 4
C 5 - 6
D 12

7. What kinds of personal characteristics do you think a good extension agent needs? Which of these characteristics do *you* have?

_____

_____

_____

EXPLORING A CAREER IN THE AGRICULTURE, FOOD & NATURAL RESOURCES CLUSTER

The O*NET program (http://online.onetcenter.org/) is the nation's primary source of occupational information. O*NET provides data on thousands of specific jobs, including typical tasks, knowledge/skills, work styles, and education required by each. Visit the O*NET site to complete this activity. (If you do not have Internet access, gather information from your library's print version of the *Occupational Outlook Handbook*.)

1. Click the Find Occupations link. In the Quick Search box, enter a job title from the Agriculture, Food & Natural Resources Career Cluster that interests you. View the Details report.

(*Note:* Sample occupations in this Career Cluster can be found at the www.careerclusters.org Web site or from your teacher.)

2. Use the information you find at O*NET to fill out the following chart for the job title you chose. List the top three characteristics of the items with an asterisk (*).

Tasks*	Tools & Technology*	Knowledge*	Skills*
Abilities*	Work Activities*	Work Context*	Interests*
Work Styles*	Work Values*	Work Needs*	Related Occupations
Education Required	Median Wages	Employment	Projected Growth

3. Would you be interested in this job? Why or why not?

_____

_____

_____